LANGUAGE AT PLAY

DIGITAL GAMES IN SECOND AND FOREIGN LANGUAGE TEACHING AND LEARNING

Julie M. Sykes
University of New Mexico

Jonathon Reinhardt
University of Arizona

Series Editors
Judith Liskin-Gasparro
Manel Lacorte

Boston Columbus Indianapolis New York San Francisco Upper Saddle River
Amsterdam Cape Town Dubai London Madrid Milan Munich Paris Montréal Toronto
Delhi Mexico City São Paulo Sydney Hong Kong Seoul Singapore Taipei Tokyo

Editor in Chief: Bob Hemmer
Editorial Assistant: Jonathan Ortiz
Senior Marketing Manager: Denise Miller
Senior Vice President: Steve Debow
Senior Managing Editor for Product Development: Mary Rottino
Associate Managing Editor: Janice Stangel
Production Manager: Fran Russello
Art Director: Jayne Conte
Cover Designer: Karen Salzbach
Full Service Production: Chitra Ganesan/PreMediaGlobal
Printer/Binder: RR Donnelley and Sons Company

Sykes, Julie M., author.
   Language at play: digital games in second and foreign language teaching and learning/
Julie M. Sykes, University of New Mexico; Jonathon Reinhardt, University of Arizona.
      pages cm
   Includes bibliographical references and index.
   ISBN-13: 978-0-205-00085-2
   ISBN-10: (invalid) 0-205-00085-1
   1. Language and languages—Study and teaching—Computer network resources.
2. Language and languages—Computer-assisted instruction. 3. Language and
languages—Study and teaching. 4. Second language acquisition—Study and teaching.
5. Human-computer interaction. 6. Educational technology. I. Reinhardt, Jonathon, author.
II. Title.
   P53.285.S95 2012
   418.0078′5—dc23

2012036301

ISBN 10: 0-205-00085-1
ISBN 13: 978-0-205-00085-2

Dedicated to our families and friends for supporting our play,
our mentors for encouraging us to play, and our fellow
gamers for teaching us how to play. Hail, Armada!
Julie & Jon

CONTENTS

PREFACE

The potential for digital games in second and foreign language teaching and learning (L2TL) is enormous. With their ever-increasing popularity for both entertainment and learning, digital games are being recognized as new contexts, spaces, and means for L2TL that were previously unimaginable. Harnessing their potential for application in the future L2 classroom, however, presents complex challenges. Instructors will need to develop appropriate pedagogical frameworks for these technologies, and researchers must analyze their potential for L2TL. Likewise, administrators will have to evaluate the practicalities of their implementation, and game designers must become familiar with language acquisition principles to bring them to the design and creation of digital games. This addition to the *Theory and Practice in Second Language Classroom Instruction* series responds to these needs by offering instructors, administrators, researchers, and game designers the information and inspiration needed to inform, enhance, and transform language learning contexts via digital games.

In this book, we offer a theoretically grounded, practical discussion of five major concepts familiar to L2TL professionals, selected because of their striking parallels in digital game design theory and second language acquisition (SLA) research. These five central concepts—goal, interaction, feedback, context, and motivation—provide the organizational structure for the book. In this preface, we present our intended purpose for the book and a discussion of who might benefit from reading it, followed by a summary of the contents of the book and suggestions for its use.

OUR PURPOSE

The overarching purpose of this volume is to provide a useful, research-based approach for understanding the intersection of L2TL research and digital games from several perspectives that have not been previously combined. In doing so, we address the growing demand for interdisciplinary frameworks, a need often voiced by L2 researchers, practitioners, and administrators. Our primary objectives are both theoretical and practical. In this book, we aim to:

1. Highlight ways digital games can inform, enhance, and ultimately transform L2 pedagogy. To this end, we address, and draw parallels among, five major concepts familiar to L2TL practitioners and digital game designers—goal, interaction, feedback, context, and motivation—to provide potentially useful analytic and pedagogical frameworks. This objective reflects our premise that research and practice should drive the adoption of any technological tool.
2. Frame our understanding of digital games in terms of the behaviors, practices, and cultures associated with their use. In doing so, we also highlight the importance of new literacies related to digital games and

caution against viewing technologically mediated spaces as merely practice or proxy environments that lead to something more important.

3. Combine multiple perspectives related to L2TL, games and learning, and
game design with the hope of starting on common ground as we move
forward. It is our view that interdisciplinary inquiry is critical to successful
research and implementation of digital games in L2TL.

4. Provide a resource to serve as a starting point for those working in
L2TL and digital games. With this goal in mind, we include information
that will be basic to some and completely new to others, depending
on their perspective and background. For example, a game designer
might find the L2TL theory completely new but the games studies information a basic summary; we might expect the reverse from an L2TL
researcher.

5. Present the complexity of issues related to digital game-mediated L2TL
in a practical and accessible manner to promote pedagogy and advocate research in this nascent field. To this end, we present readers with
multiple comparisons, contrasts, and perspectives; synthesized and imple-
mentable conceptual frameworks; feasible and understandable scenarios;
and opportunities for reflection and application.

WILL THIS BOOK BE USEFUL FOR YOU?

Our overarching goal for this book is to introduce the concept of **digital game-
mediated L2TL** to a broad audience. By *digital*, we mean any game that is
played through a desktop computer, laptop computer, tablet, game console
(e.g., Xbox, PlayStation), handheld game console (e.g., Nintendo DS), or other
mobile device (e.g., iPod Touch, cell phone). By *game*, we refer to digital
games of a variety of genres and types, from action-adventure to simulation-
management games, from single to multiplayer, and from mini-games played
on mobile devices (e.g., *Angry Birds*) to massively multiplayer online games
(e.g., *World of Warcraft*). We cover this diversity in Appendix II: Guide to
Game Types and Genres. Please note that the term *game* in this book is used to
refer to digital game, for the sake of brevity.

The terms *mediated* and *L2TL* reflect particular theoretical perspectives,
which we explore in the background section of Chapter 1. Briefly, *mediated*
recognizes that games are a tool or medium for facilitating L2 teaching and
learning. This important distinction reflects our sociocultural perspective that
focuses on the role of mediation in learning. We also use the acronym *L2TL*
to refer to second or foreign language teaching and learning. We believe that
teaching can happen with or without the presence of a human teacher, because
teaching techniques and pedagogical principles are often designed into tools
such as workbooks, textbooks, and games. We prefer the term *learning* to acquisition, because we believe that learning is developmental in nature; involves
participation, internalization, and socialization; and is not only an individual
phenomenon (Block, 2003; Reinhardt, 2012).

To further outline the concept of digital game-mediated L2TL, we explore five concepts—goal, interaction, feedback, context, and motivation—that are fundamental to both L2TL and digital game design. We utilize a variety of perspectives in applied linguistics, educational gaming, and games studies, some of which will be familiar to the reader, others new. Because our primary audience is L2TL practitioners, we frame each chapter with practice-related scenarios in multiple languages and provide integrated opportunities for reflection and evaluation. However, our intention is that this approachable structure will be appropriate for anyone interested in the intersection of L2TL and digital gaming. This audience includes the following:

- *Pre- and in-service L2 instructors.* Through the liberal use of scenarios, practical examples, and reflection questions, we hope to inform instructors and inspire them to consider digital game-mediated L2 instruction as a possible curricular component for the near future.
- *L2 curriculum and materials developers.* Developers, or instructors in a developer role, will find this book useful. In the text, we offer examples of, and ideas for, integrating digital games into L2 materials. We also include questions for reflection and discussion that we hope will inspire creative new ideas for classroom materials design.
- *Administrators.* For administrators, lab directors, and information technology (IT) personnel, the volume will be useful as a reference text with advantageous frameworks, a glossary, a game typology, and a game evaluation guide.

Most ambitiously, our intention is for the volume to be useful for those researching L2TL and digital games, as well as for those designing and building digital games for L2TL purposes.

- *Researchers.* This book will be useful for researchers because it is among the first to integrate educational gaming and games studies research with applied linguistics and L2 pedagogy research. As such, we intend each chapter as a starting point to spark ideas for future research. In addition, a deeper understanding of the practical issues associated with design and implementation can aid researchers in selecting relevant research topics related to L2TL. Each chapter concludes with ideas for research, and the book includes an extensive reference section for additional reading.
- *Digital game designers and developers.* Professionals in digital game design and development will find in the volume an approach unlike most in their field because it is written by two applied linguists bridging into digital games, rather than by digital game theorists attempting to approach L2TL with little grounding in the discourses of our field. Although our primary audience is the L2TL community, and we make no pretense to expertise in professional digital game design and development, we believe we may offer a fresh voice to some in those fields.

Whatever your background or perspective, we encourage you to select the elements most useful for your endeavors.

YOUR REFLECTIONS

Throughout this book, you will find multiple opportunities to stop and reflect on what you have read and integrate it with your understandings and experiences. This reflection experience can be as informal as pausing to consider each of the questions as an individual or as formal as a journal in which you keep written reflections and notes. We strongly encourage collaboration and discussion of the questions with others if the opportunity arises, as we see collaborative learning and discussion as vital to the issues raised through these reflection questions. No matter the approach you choose, we encourage you to consciously reflect on these questions before continuing:

1. What are your preconceptions about digital games and L2TL? Have you ever used digital games for L2TL as an instructor or learner? What potentials do you think there are?
2. Based on the little information you have about this book so far, what elements are most appealing to you? What are you hoping to gain from interacting with this volume?
3. We designed this book to be relevant to five primary audiences: instructors, materials developers, administrators, researchers, and game designers. Which reader group(s) do you belong to? What areas of the book are most pertinent to your reader perspective(s)?

CONTENTS OF THE BOOK

In this book, readers will find theoretical discussions and practical examples relevant to digital games for L2TL. Each of the five body chapters discusses a concept central to L2TL and familiar to practitioners and researchers. In addition to the main text, various resources guide the reader to a more thorough understanding of the parallel concept being discussed. These include

- *Scenarios.* An opening scenario and game-mediated scenario are included in each chapter to contextualize the main concepts and present the issues from a variety of perspectives, including those of the teacher, student, and administrator.
- *Reflection Questions.* Questions for consideration are included after each major section of the chapter. We encourage readers to explore these questions prior to moving forward with the next section. Our hope is that the questions will spark additional discussion, provide food for thought, and encourage debate on the central issues of the book.
- *Summary and Implications.* At the conclusion of each chapter, we highlight the main ideas that have been presented.
- *Game-Mediated Activity Examples.* Activities that can be used in L2TL are included with the intention that they can be adapted as models by instructors and researchers. We offer activities from a game-enhanced, game-based, and game-informed perspective that highlights the main concepts from each chapter.

- *Suggested Readings*. We present suggestions for further reading at the end of the book. These are annotated to help readers select the resources most relevant for their own interests. We have included readings from L2TL theory, game-mediated L2TL research, and games studies.
- *Appendices*. Three appendices are included to add additional details related to the concepts central to the book. Appendix I: Glossary presents definitions of the boldfaced concepts and terms included throughout the book. Appendix II: Guide to Game Types and Genres is a summary of the most popular digital game genres and types. Appendix III: Digital Game Evaluation Guide for L2TL offers an evaluation guide for the selection of digital games based on the central premises of each of the main chapters.

Chapter 1 presents relevant background information to inform our discussion of each of the five primary topics in Chapters 2–6. This includes brief exploration of perspectives on learning, games, and play, as well as a review of the theoretical premises that inform the book. We also present a taxonomy for discussing digital games and review previous work in digital games and L2TL.

Chapter 2, **Goals**, explores the first parallel in L2TL and digital games through a focus on goal orientation and its relationship to the concept of *task*. In this chapter, we first examine the various conceptualizations of L2 learning tasks and the multiple characterizations of task-based learning and teaching (TBLT). This is followed by a discussion of the criticisms of task-based L2TL from a game-informed perspective. Insights include the need to separate task from activity; to reexamine the notion of authenticity in light of learners' experiences; and to refocus on learner-driven task design, as opposed to instructor-driven task design. We then explore goal orientation from the game design perspective. Here we address the ways in which digital game playing exhibits goal-orienting behavior, the design of various types of digital game tasks and objectives, and ways in which tasks help shape a multiplicity of play experiences (e.g., open-ended play and linear play). Ultimately, the chapter highlights the importance of dynamic task design through a goal-orienting perspective in which L2TL goals and tasks are learner driven and continuously negotiated to create engaging and meaningful L2TL experiences.

Interaction is the focus of Chapter 3 and is the second parallel explored in this book. Utilizing the opening scenario, we begin with a brief discussion of the social and interactive nature of digital games. We then highlight the importance of interaction in L2TL, including central concepts such as negotiation for meaning and Halliday's (1978) model of ideational, interpersonal, and textual meaning as applied to interaction. This is followed by an analysis of game-mediated L2 interaction—ideational interaction with games, interpersonal interaction through and around games, and textual interaction about games. We also examine interaction from a game design perspective, highlighting the parallel concepts of cognitive interactivity (i.e., what happens in the player's mind during the gameplay experience), functional interactivity (i.e., the game interface and physical interactivity with the game), explicit interactivity (i.e., designed in-game structures centered on choice and decision making by the player), and cultural interactivity (i.e., interaction around digital games via associated attendant discourses; Salen & Zimmerman,

2004). Game designers demonstrate the importance of a good interactive design that is promoted through immersive experiences, ergonomic interfaces, discernable integrated choices, and connections to the world outside the game. In this chapter, we focus on how these principles are useful for L2TL as well.

Chapter 4 entails a discussion of **feedback** and the numerous game-informed insights that can enhance L2TL. In digital games, players are provided with consistent, individualized assistance at just the right time to be able to continue progressing. In this way, games promote both short-term experimentation and failure in order to promote long-term mastery. We begin the chapter with an analysis of feedback as instruction in L2TL, highlighting the concepts of comprehensible input, scaffolding and the zone of proximal development, and language learning strategies. This is followed by a discussion of the challenges often associated with feedback in L2TL—fear of failure, time constraints, language variation, and lack of social consequence and internalization. We then analyze feedback in digital games, including the importance of fail states (i.e., points in a game that facilitate failure to help the learner gain the skills necessary to continue through real-time feedback); individualized, just-in-time feedback; types of feedback; and feedback via associated digital game communities. Throughout the chapter, we emphasize implications for L2TL.

Context, a critical element of L2TL and digital games, is the focus of Chapter 5. Although we focus on the designed contexts of both digital games spaces and L2 instructional units, we also emphasize the context surrounding the designed experiences, that is, context-in-the-game and context of play. The chapter begins with a discussion of context in L2TL and linguistics more broadly. We then focus on narrative as a contextualization mechanism for learning and an underlying principle of game design. In the chapter, we highlight the importance of game-mediated narratives, both designed and personal, as resources for additional contextualization of L2TL.

Chapter 6 addresses the complex topic of **motivation** by integrating insights from previous chapters. We first offer a summary of several models of motivation in L2TL, for example, Gardner and Lambert's concept of integrative and instrumental orientation (Gardner & Lambert, 1972), Dörnyei's (2005) L2 motivational self model, and models of motivation from the sociocultural perspective. This is followed by an analysis of player and game motivation in digital games. We emphasize the importance of flow states in motivation as well as engagement as a driving design force. The chapter further highlights motivation in digital games as one element that is part of a larger system that includes goal orientation, interaction, feedback, and context. We highlight ways digital games have the potential to increase motivation in L2TL through meaningful gameplay, community engagement, and game-informed pedagogy.

We conclude the book in Chapter 7 with a summary of the main premises of the volume and a brief discussion of the future of digital game-mediated L2TL. Game-informed L2TL has great potential for enhancing, and potentially transforming, the L2 learning experience. This book is just the tip of the iceberg in terms of possible future applications of digital games in L2TL practice and research. As you read, we encourage you to reflect on the issues presented, consider your own ideas for practice and research, and play, play, play!

Introduction

In this chapter, we introduce a number of concepts fundamental to our discussion of the parallels between second language teaching and learning (L2TL) and games. Although our particular theoretical perspectives on L2TL will become clearer with discussion of the parallels, we begin by orienting ourselves theoretically by posing three big questions. Then, we present our framework for conceptualizing game-mediated L2TL by discussing the concepts of game-enhanced and game-based. We conclude the chapter with a brief discussion of current research on digital game-mediated L2TL. As you read, we encourage you to stop and ponder the "Your reflections" questions that are at the end of each section.

1.1 LANGUAGE, GAMES, PLAY, AND LEARNING

We first consider three big questions:

- What is language?
- What is play?
- What is a game?

These broad questions lead to a fourth on how game playing is related to learning. Although readers may consider other legitimate perspectives on these ideas, our perspectives serve as a theoretical foundation for the ideas we introduce throughout the book.

1.1.1 What is language?

Language is first and foremost a way of making social meaning and is ultimately about communicating with others. Language is made real through use, and social interaction is key to this activity. Thus, in agreement with M. A. K. Halliday

(1978), we view language as a social-semiotic phenomenon. Linguistic structure is not separate from meaning, but rather, meaning emerges dynamically through language use. Learning is a sociocultural activity, as noted by Vygotsky (1978) and Lantolf and Thorne (2006), mediated by linguistic and cultural semiosis—that is, sign making and interpretation. Language learning happens through the interplay of the social and the cognitive (e.g., Atkinson, 2002) and is inseparable from enculturation (e.g., Duff, 2008; Ochs & Schieffelin, 1984). Social activity is key to learning, and using language in socially meaningful ways is the way to develop the most comprehensive repertoire.

1.1.2 What is play?

A notable social activity is **play**, a human (and animal) activity that has been studied by biologists, anthropologists, sociologists, and linguists throughout history (e.g., Huizinga, 1938). It is fundamental to our nature. A basic distinction is often made between *ludus*, or rule-bound play, and *paidia*, or open-ended, free play. Caillois (1961) noted that play can also involve *mimesis*, mimicry or imitation; *ilinx*, vertigo or movement; *agon*, competition; and *alea*, chance. All of these are activities we can easily identify in games. Scholars note, however, that these activities alone do not make play, but that play is a matter of the player's disposition, or the acknowledgment that these activities happen within a particular bounded time and place, where the rules are different from those of the world outside the game.

   Play is associated with development, and psychologists have noted the importance of a playful disposition for growth and learning. Similarly, applied linguists have theorized that **language play**, or playing with the formal qualities of language (i.e., disassociating it from conventional meaning), may facilitate learning (Cook, 2000; Crystal, 2001; Lantolf, 1997). Language play by second language (L2) learners during speaking (Bell, 2005; Pomerantz & Bell, 2007), writing (Belz, 2002), or online chat (Belz & Reinhardt, 2004) may aid learning by drawing attention to language form and may relate to identity development (Belz, 2002). Although language play does not necessarily always occur in digital games, game-mediated L2TL environments can be designed to promote a playful disposition and the language play that comes with it.

1.1.3 What is a game?

A game is a unique kind of activity around which we often find play. As such, a game reflects a set of cultural practices through which players make social meaning and, in Schell's words, is truly defined by the *imaginary experience* (2008, pp. 10–11). In many cases, games are easy to identify yet difficult to define, a task many games theorists have been attempting to do for quite some time. Here, we are not attempting to settle any debate about what is and is not a game. Instead, we aim to highlight the most salient characteristics of games as central elements critical for game-mediated L2TL. Game theorist Jesper Juul (2005) defines a **game** as necessarily being rule based; having outcomes that are variable, quantifiable, and valorized; involving player effort and attachment to outcomes; and having negotiable consequences. Utilizing a different approach, Schell (2008) ultimately defines games as "a problem solving activity, approached with a playful attitude" (p. 37), yet he discusses many of the same qualities of games proposed by Juul. As a *problem-solving activity*, games are entered willfully; have goals, conflict, and rules; can be won and lost; are interactive; have challenges; create their own internal value; engage players; and are closed, formal systems (Schell, 2008). Taking these two converging approaches, we can say that:

- A player voluntarily plays a game knowing he or she is bound by a set of rules (these can be followed or flouted).
- Games require effort to reach a goal (this goal can be open ended or clearly defined, yet it is always ultimately authenticated by the player).
- Games will often result in a variety of differing outcomes, some better than others.
- Games create an internally rewarding system.

The ways in which these characteristics emerge is distinct for any game-playing experience. For example, a game may support effort and reduce challenge in difficult areas by scaffolding particular actions, giving the player just what he/she needs when he/she needs it. Moreover, in some games, players play against each other and there is a clear winner and loser; in others, such as simulations, they play against themselves so to speak, and there is no endpoint of victory or defeat. Ultimately, when defining games, it seems most useful to examine the game play experiences and behaviors that characterize the unmistakable identification of activity that is a game.

1.1.4 How is gameplay related to learning?

As mentioned earlier, our view of language is as a social semiotic, coherent with socio-cognitive and sociocultural views of learning. With regard to digital game-mediated L2TL, we emphasize the social nature of language, games, play, and learning. From this perspective, we recognize gameplay as (1) a social practice and a new form of literacy and (2) a productive model for game-informed pedagogy that can transform language learning experiences.

First, **game literacy** (Gee, 2007), the ability to play, learn through, and understand games, can be considered a *new digital literacy* (Lankshear & Knobel, 2006; Thorne, 2012), an aspect of multiliteracies (New London Group, 1996). Reinhardt and Thorne (2011) note that from this new perspective:

> Becoming literate in a particular semiotic practice (or set of practices) requires the ability to interpret and generate signs that are meaningful to a community of practice (Lave & Wenger, 1991), while it also involves the development of an identity appropriate to that practice (Gee, 2004).

Digital gaming, mediated through language and other semiotic means such as images, sounds, and movements, is an activity many people use to create meaning, on their own and with others as a social practice. Many games have **attendant discourses** in the form of websites and other literacy practices produced by player communities—players create and draw on these discourses as they play. In other words, players develop game literacy by experiencing various games and participating in attendant discursive practices, as well as by analyzing these game-mediated literacy practices with a critically aware disposition. Gameplay becomes part of their identity. Expert gamers do not just know how to play; they have developed intricate knowledge about the structures, principles, and mechanisms involved in game design. Some researchers (e.g., Steinkuehler, 2007) even argue that digital gaming not only makes players better at understanding or designing games, but also helps them develop dispositions toward learning and literacy that go beyond gaming. These skills are an aspect of the new digital literacies we all need to thrive in the future.

Digital game behaviors also have a great deal of potential for game-informed L2TL. This includes attention to the social nature of learning that often accompanies gameplay with attention to connections for various L2 learning contexts. Throughout this book, we highlight five major areas in which digital games can inform L2TL—goal orienting, interaction, feedback, context, and motivation. Each area presents promising applications to language learning.

1.1.5 Your reflections

1. Do you agree with the definition of language as a social semiotic? How else might you define language?
2. What do you think is the most important feature of the definition of *game*? In other words, what makes a game a game?
3. What do you think are the cognitive, social, and cultural functions of *play*? In other words, what is its purpose?
4. What experiences do you have with language play? Do you think it is an important aspect of language learning?
5. What are some other new digital literacies involving new technologies? How might these be related to gameplay experiences?
6. Are there any behaviors in games you have played that you see as especially interesting for L2TL?

1.2 GAME-ENHANCED AND GAME-BASED L2TL

In any emerging field, it can be extremely beneficial to have a heuristic or taxonomy to help conceptualize main themes and direction. Here, we add to our understanding of *game-mediated L2TL* by making basic distinction between *game-enhanced L2TL* and *game-based L2TL*. Originally described in Reinhardt and Sykes (2012), we utilize this framework as an organizing principle for the activities and concepts discussed throughout the volume.

Game-enhanced L2TL is the application of vernacular games in L2TL. **Vernacular games** are those not designed for educational purposes, the ones available commercially online or on a disc, from a store or the developer. They are produced around the world; exist in dozens of languages; and can be played on local computers, consoles, handheld devices, and via web-based applications (see Appendix II: Guide to Game Types and Genres for examples). Game-enhanced research seeks to investigate "how vernacular games can afford L2 learning and

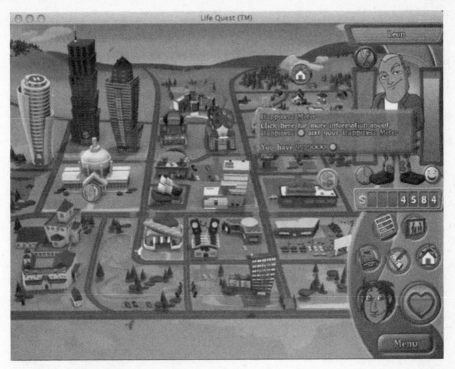

FIGURE 1.1 LifeQuest Big Fish Games, 2011.

how those affordances might be realized in formal pedagogical environments" (Reinhardt & Sykes, 2012, p. 37). For example, in what ways might the casual game LifeQuest (see Figure 1.1), be useful for the teaching and learning of English? In this game, players compete with their high school rivals to get the best education, job, living space, and partner. The narrative and focal lexical and grammatical content offer great potential for game-enhanced L2TL. Key questions focusing on game-enhanced L2TL ask how game-mediated L2 learning happens in informal, noneducational environments and, therefore, how vernacular games might be employed for formal, educational purposes.

In addition to the use of vernacular games, we have the opportunity to design, teach, and learn with games created specifically with teaching and learning in mind. With this understanding, we define **game-based** L2TL as "the use of games and game-inclusive synthetic immersive environments that are designed intentionally for L2 learning and pedagogy. The purpose of game-based L2TL research is to inform the evaluation and design of these games and environments" (Reinhardt & Sykes, 2012, p. 39). **Game-based environments** are especially useful for targeting specific language features that, in many instances, are not feasible to address via traditional classroom practices. For example, Croquelandia is a synthetic immersive environment that explicitly targets the acquisition of requests and apologies in Spanish (see Figure 1.2).

In addition, game-based environments allow for the real-time collection of a comprehensive data set that can be immediately used to improve future

FIGURE 1.2 Croquelandia The player apologizes to a stranger on the street.
Source: Sykes, 2008.

iterations of the game. Key questions focusing on game-based learning and teaching ask how specific game designs afford particular L2 learner behaviors, and how game-based environments can be designed to incorporate and/or complement L2 pedagogical uses. Game-based L2TL is still in its infancy with only a handful of game-based spaces currently in existence. We summarize each in Table 1.1.

Thus far, few game-based spaces are available for L2TL, with the majority either proprietary or available on a limited basis only. At present, a number of additional spaces are being designed for the commercial and educational markets. We fully anticipate an explosion of games built explicitly for L2TL in the near future. It is critical that researchers and practitioners evaluate and, in many cases, participate in the creation of these games for L2TL. In doing so, they ensure that L2TL principles, rather than market demands, drive game design. This book is one step toward making this collaboration a reality.

In our original description of the framework (Reinhardt & Sykes, 2012), we caution against the tendency to view game-based L2TL as superior to game-enhanced L2TL because of its explicit educational focus for three reasons:

1. There are reasons for researching L2 learning in, and teaching with, vernacular games that cannot be replicated with L2TL-purposed games. For example, as a result of their prolific existence globally, vernacular games afford learners the potential to develop literacies and related identities through participation in international, often multilingual, communities. It would be

Table 1.1 Summary of game-based environments for L2TL

Digital Game-Based Environment	Language	Description	Availability Status
Croquelandia	Spanish	A synthetic immersive environment specifically created for the learning of Spanish pragmatics (i.e., apologies and requests); learners complete a series of quests that guide them through apologizing and requesting in a variety of contexts.	Research prototype only
Language Island	Arabic English French German Italian Japanese Korean Mandarin Portuguese Spanish	A virtual world developed for young learners of foreign languages; functioning much like an online amusement park with various games, group adventures, storytelling, and a multilingual chat feature. http://languageislandblog.blogspot.com/	Demo only
Mentira	Spanish	A place-based, augmented reality mobile game in which learners must search for clues in both a virtual neighborhood and an existing physical neighborhood to solve a murder mystery; learners utilize a mobile device to interact with a Spanish-speaking neighborhood in Albuquerque, NM. http://www.mentira.org	Open-source code for development in ARIS; freely available online from iTunes via the ARIS application; need an iOS device for play.
MIDDWorld Online	French Spanish	A first-person online role playing game (RPG) that immerses players in environments unique to each language's specific culture. Students will interact with other players and with computer-controlled characters who are voiced by native speakers. http://www.middleburyinteractive.com/story.php?id=13	Proprietary version available for French I and Spanish I.

(continued)

Table 1.1 (Continued)

Digital Game-Based Environment	Language	Description	Availability Status
Tactical Language and Culture Training Systems	Arabic Dari French Pashto	Immersive 3-D environments that teach language and culture skills for defense situations; include training and practice phases with a focus on voice recognition. http://www.alelo.com/tactical_language.html	Restricted; available for purchase by primarily military entities.
Zon	Mandarin	A two-dimensional virtual world developed at Michigan State University; offers a comprehensive built-in syllabus structure similar to an introductory textbook; learners embark on a journey to China and must interact with non-player characters to complete various activities. http://enterzon.com/	Online access; freely available for play.

Source: Adapted from Reinhardt and Sykes (2012).

difficult to create similar communities with game-based environments. We believe that the pedagogical use of vernacular games is underexplored, and that game-enhanced L2TL pedagogies should continue to be developed, implemented, and assessed.

2. Not all L2TL-purposed educational games are, or should be, all encompassing. We believe the potential and need are great for L2TL-purposed games targeted at particular L2TL areas, and that we should be thoughtful and judicious about their application. Moreover, they should be designed to integrate with, not replace, larger L2TL environments. We contest the implication that game-based environments might somehow be able to replace teachers; their teaching and assessment expertise; and their vast stores of pedagogical, practical, and content knowledge.

3. On a related note, we believe that a multiplicity of resource types is more efficacious for L2TL, no matter how comprehensive a single resource might be. Games will never replace all L2TL activities and should not be considered an end-all-be-all for language learning. For example, a game, no matter how engaging, all encompassing, or immersive, can never replicate the real-world experience of study abroad, and the emergent and contingent learning that it brings. Some learners may never respond to a game, no matter how well designed the game may be; for those learners, other resources are needed.

In reality, the research and practice of both game-enhanced and game-based L2TL are critical and complement each other. Researchers and developers of game-based applications must be aware of game-enhanced practice and research, as well as the benefits of working with vernacular games for L2TL. Likewise, those working in the area of game-enhanced L2TL should be aware of the educationally focused digital games available, the benefits of those applications, and how game-enhanced and game-based research and practice may inform their ongoing development.

1.2.1 Your reflections

1. What are the advantages and disadvantages of a game-enhanced focus for L2TL? A game-based focus?
2. Have you played in a game-based environment for L2TL? If so, what was your experience like? If not, what do you think it might be like?
3. How does research inform practice, and vice versa? What are some areas that you think might be worth researching with regard to game-enhanced or game-based practice?

1.3 DIGITAL GAME-MEDIATED L2TL: WHAT HAS BEEN DONE?

Concurrent with the games and learning movement in education, we have witnessed an increasing number of studies addressing the use of digital games in L2TL. The majority of this work is theoretical in nature and addresses both game-enhanced and game-based L2TL, using a variety of heuristics and methodologies. A comprehensive discussion of each individual study related to game-mediated L2TL is beyond the scope of this book and outside its primary focus. We have, however, provided a comprehensive list of references and a selected annotated reading list to guide anyone interested in more in-depth treatment of the issues discussed here.

The theoretical work that has been produced up to this points focuses primarily on the benefits of different types of game-mediated spaces (Sykes, Oskoz, & Thorne, 2008), situating game-based learning in the area of language learning (Thomas, 2012), specific discussions of goal-orientation and feedback in both game-enhanced and game-based environments (Sykes, Reinhardt, & Thorne, 2010), principles of game-mediated design for L2TL (Purushotma, Thorne, & Wheatley, 2008), the role of digital games as related to communities for L2TL (Filsecker & Bündgens-Kosten, 2012; Sykes & Holden, 2011), and the potential for language socialization via digital game-enhanced pedagogy and interaction with attendant discourses (Thorne, Black, & Sykes, 2009; Reinhardt & Zander, 2011). Each presents one perspective on the many potential benefits of game-mediated L2TL.

In the area of game-enhanced L2TL using vernacular, off-the-shelf digital games, a number of relevant studies have recently emerged. These include empirical studies of language learning via commercial game spaces. Researchers have addressed the use of guilds in massively multiplayer online games (MMOGs— see Appendix II for a description) for social and collaborative work related to language learning (Bryant, 2006; Peterson, 2012) and discourse of collaborative gameplay as related to L2TL (Reinders & Wattana, 2012; Piiranen-Marsh & Tainio, 2009), ecological psychology (Zheng, Young, Wagner, & Brewer, 2009), cognitive load theory (deHaan, Reed, & Kuwada, 2010), vocabulary acquisition (Purushotma, 2005; Sundqvist & Kerstin Sylvén, 2012), and language socialization (Reinhardt & Zander, 2011; Thorne, 2008). In terms of game-based L2TL using digital games built specifically for language learning, researchers have examined the construction of narrative structures (Neville, 2010), L2 pragmatic development (Sykes, 2008, 2009), corrective feedback (Cornillie, Desmot, and Clarebout, 2012), learner behavior patterns (Sykes, 2010), and place-based learning via mobile games (Holden & Sykes, 2011). Each is just a starting point for work in this area, but together, they begin to form an interesting body of work related to game-enhanced L2TL.

Based on a review of this theoretical work (see Table 1.2), Sykes and Holden (2011) summarize the benefits of one type of digital game—MMOGs. Although Sykes and Holden discuss only MMOGs, each of the characteristics is also relevant for other game genres and types, including game-based environments. These characteristics are explored in more detail throughout the various chapters of this volume.

Table 1.2 Potential benefits of MMOGs

Characteristic	Description	References
Goal Orientation and Goal-Directed Activity	Parallel to a task-based approach to language learning, quest completion forms the underlying architecture of gameplay in MMOGs. By completing quests, players are rewarded with experience and items in the game. Players make choices from hundreds of quests and must often work with others who have complementary skills for successful completion.	Gee (2007); Purushotma et al. (2008); Sykes et al. (2010)
Social Consequence and Interconnectedness	MMOGs are high-stakes, meaningful spaces with social consequences for the players and their relationships with others. Although the tasks themselves have little real-world impact beyond the fantasy space of the game, the collaborative behaviors and social relationships are very real and meaningful.	Nardi, Ly, and Harris (2007); Purushotma et al. (2008); Squire and Steinkuehler (2006); Sykes et al. (2010); Thorne and Black (2007); Thorne et al. (2009)
Potential for Language Socialization	Gameplay and participation in MMOG communities lead learners toward increasingly complex, dynamic, and intimate relationships related to both in-game and about-game contexts.	Nardi et al. (2007); Squire and Steinkuehler (2006); Thorne and Black, 2007; Thorne et al. (2009)

Characteristic	Description	References
Complex, Meaningful Feedback	Feedback is given to players at multiple levels in meaningful ways, making experimentation and fail states critical to successful advancement and skill building.	Gee (2007); Purushotma et al. (2008); Sykes et al. (2010)
Engagement	Players are immersed in the gameplay activity and, although challenging, find the experiences to be rewarding long term.	Purushotma et al. (2008)

Source: Adapted from Sykes and Holden (2011, p. 319).

1.3.1 Your reflections

1. Does the research presented here fit with your ideas about digital games and L2TL? Why or why not?
2. What is the purpose of theoretical and empirical research in a new field such as game-mediated L2TL?
3. What are some notable areas missing from this emergent body of research?

1.4 MOVING AHEAD

In this chapter, we have briefly discussed the underlying theoretical constructs informing this book. A general summary of the main points from this introductory chapter follows:

1. Language is a way of making social meaning and is ultimately about communicating with others. It is inseparable from enculturation and social activity is key to learning.
2. Play occurs in bounded time and space and is an important construct when considering game-mediated L2TL. Games can be designed to promote a playful disposition and the learning that often comes with it.
3. Games are ultimately about problem solving with a playful disposition. Some common characteristics include voluntary play, a set of rules, effort, challenge, salient goals, varying outcomes, and internally rewarding systems.
4. Game playing is (a) a social practice and new form of literacy worthy of our attention and (b) a productive model for the design of game-informed pedagogy.
5. Game-mediated L2TL can be characterized using a framework that makes the distinction between game-enhanced L2TL and game-based L2TL.
6. Research on game-mediated L2TL is still in its infancy; however, we are now able to draw some general conclusions to inform future work.

Throughout the remainder of this book, we will consider many of these issues in more detail and draw on our understanding here to inform more detailed discussions. In Chapter 2, we begin with the first parallel concept and a fundamental component of digital games—goals.

CHAPTER **2**

■ ■ ■ ■ ■

Goals
Learning tasks
and goal orientation

2.1 A SCENARIO: *THE THIEF IN THE MUSEUM*

Profesor Martín

In an intermediate-level Spanish classroom, Profesor Martín has created a con-textualized task consisting of several activities for learning the subjunctive. He first presents a story from the news describing the circumstances of an actual burglary recently committed in a Spanish museum and then leads a brief dis-cussion about the incident and a painting that was stolen. The class is then divided into groups of three to complete an information jigsaw task. The stu-dents are given handouts with different fictional information for each group member. Each sheet lists a series of invented facts, suspect descriptions, and bits of evidence, from which the students are supposed to work together to make predictions about who committed the crime and what might have hap-pened. Profesor Martín instructs the students to discuss the information and write five sentences using the phrases of doubt, possibility, suspicion, and importance that he has written on the board. He believes this will aid them in practicing the subjunctive mood in a meaningful way. However, the activity does not turn out as intended. Instead of engaging in meaningful commu-nication to complete the task, each learner approached the task differently, and many did not complete the task successfully. Some resorted to English to be sure they had the right answers. He is looking forward to taking a new approach that allows for a more meaningful level of student involvement next time.

The Students

Erica, Mateo, Lillian, and Roland start out excited about class and about perfect-ing their skills. However, the day does not turn out as they had hoped. While doing a mystery activity prepared by Profesor Martín, Erica's group became distracted by several vocabulary words in their suspect descriptions. They had time only to look up the words and write them down in their notes. Erica is worried because they finished only three sentences. Mateo's group completed two sentences but then agreed that the painting that was stolen was ugly and it did not matter that it was stolen. They ended up talking, instead, about what they had for lunch. Lillian's group was frustrated with the difficulty of the task right away so, instead, wrote two sentences accusing fellow class members of stealing the paintings. Roland's group gave all the sheets to the smartest student, who wrote five correct statements, which the others copied. Overall, the students generally knew what they were supposed to do, and some produced the appropriate outcome; however, Erica, Mateo, Lillian, and Roland all expressed a lack of interest in, or frustration with, the activity.

2.1.1 Scenario questions

1. What pedagogical approach is the instructor using? What do you think of the activities leading up to the main jigsaw tasks? What do you think of the primary jigsaw task? What are its strengths and weaknesses? Have you done similar activity sequences with students? If so, what were they like? Have you done them as a learner yourself? If so, what were they like?
2. What does the instructor intend for the learners to learn from the activity? What do you think they actually learn?
3. In another implementation of the same scenario, perhaps in a different context, the task could have resulted in the intended outcome. What might the instructor have done to encourage the outcome he wanted in this implementation?

This classroom activity presents a worst-case L2TL scenario that could very well have turned out differently. Often, well-designed, well-intentioned tasks such as this one do result in the intended outcomes, but many times they do not. In this chapter, we explore how a game-informed perspective might alter, and even add to, our understanding of the presented scenario. As is the case throughout this book, we do not mean to imply that game-mediated activities are unequivocally superior to those that are not; rather, considering the same sort of activity from a game-informed perspective provides insight into how, and why, outcomes could be different and, in many cases, improved.

2.2 TASKS AND L2TL

In this chapter, we explore the first area in which L2 learning experiences and environments may benefit from further understanding of digital games—goal orientation and its relationship to the concept of *task*. Whereas most can see the parallels in game playing and L2 learning in that both are goal-oriented activities, the term *task*, which brings to mind *work*, might seem antithetical to play and games. This is especially the case when *task* is misconstrued to mean the same as **activity**, a common misconception we explore in detail shortly. In fact, the cultural assumption that learning should be hard work, or else it is not really learning, is deeply ingrained. Yet, it is not the reality in many cases. It is a misconception to believe, consciously or not, that play is antithetical to learning; we believe this misconception leads instructors, administrators, parents, and even students to brush aside games as frivolous, something better suited to free time and as a reward than as an effective way to learn. Unpacking and examining concepts such as *task* and *goal* is a step toward this understanding.

To this end, in this chapter, we first examine the theoretical perspectives on task-based language teaching (TBLT) and the definition of L2 learning task. This is followed by a game-informed discussion of some of the criticisms of the notion. We then explore goal orientation as a crucial aspect of game design and the game-playing experience with insights for L2TL. The chapter concludes with a summary of the main points and implications for game-informed L2TL, followed by a new scenario and ideas for teaching and research. As you read, we encourage you to stop and ponder the "Your reflections" questions at the end of the sections.

2.2.1 TBLT and defining L2 learning tasks

Since the advent of communicative language teaching (Savignon, 1972) several decades ago, the concept of **task** has been at the heart of L2TL. Communicative language teaching places a strong focus on the communicative functions of language and, as a result, emphasizes production for various functional purposes in the classroom (for a historical account of the emergence of communicative language teaching and task-based approaches, see Brown, 2007; Omaggio Hadley, 2001; Richards & Rodgers, 2001). Historically, however, the primary emphasis in many communicative language teaching classrooms has remained on discrete components of language (e.g., lexical items, morphemes) that are primarily form focused. Drawing on many fundamental characteristics of communicative language teaching, **task-based language teaching** (TBLT) emerged as an approach centered on functional language use not only as a central component of the classroom, but also as a critical driving force for syllabus design and assessment (Van den Branden, Bygate, & Norris, 2009).

There are several different schools of thought regarding TBLT (e.g., Ellis, 2003; Nunan, 1989, 2004; Prabhu, 1987; Skehan, 1998; Willis, 1996). In general, most agree that an L2 classroom task focuses primarily on meaning for language use in the real world. A task is focused on a goal and should be authentic, that is, be similar to something that people do with language outside of the classroom. When ideal task conditions are met, learning will predictably occur, based on sound Second Language Acquisition (SLA) principles. Success of such tasks is then measured based on their outcomes. As we will discuss shortly, the authenticity of tasks ultimately results from the learner's use of them. Therefore, throughout our discussion, we must be cognizant of the varying experiences that occur with the same task. Nevertheless, the target of task design in TBLT is what people do with language outside of the classroom. Despite the overarching similarities found in the majority of approaches to TBLT, varying perspectives emerge when addressing the ideal task conditions. This also has an impact on the ways in which tasks are integrated in the curriculum, as well as the type and intensity of attention paid to form.

In what Skehan (1998) deems a *weak* form of TBLT, tasks are central to the pedagogical process but may also be superseded by explicit instruction and practice as necessary to ensure a sufficient focus on form. Included in this cognitive perspective would also be what Samuda and Bygate (2008) consider *task-supported language teaching* and *task-referenced language teaching*. From this perspective, task is seen as merely a basic unit for assessable L2TL classroom activity that focuses on meaningful interaction. This approach recognizes an occasional need for attention to form, but never at the expense of meaning. However, in a *strong* view of TBLT, tasks comprise the primary unit of curriculum design, implementation, and assessment. From this perspective, TBLT is a comprehensive pedagogical approach with SLA theoretical entailments, "a realization of the communicative language teaching philosophy at the levels of syllabus design and methodology" (Nunan, 2004, p. 10). As such, tasks are the mechanism that drives all L2 development. From this perspective, the ideal L2 learning task is one with which learners focus on meaning rather than form. The difference between forms and form is key, because attention to forms (as countable objects) focuses more on decontextualized formal properties of language (e.g., pronunciation, grammar), whereas attention to form (as a feature or quality) focuses more on how those properties are intertwined with meaning (Doughty & Williams, 1998).

Ellis (2003) further highlights theoretical perspectives of the TBLT approach in terms of a psycholinguistic perspective (i.e., planning and task construction) and a sociocultural perspective (i.e., implementation of tasks and interactions during tasks). The distinction is an important one that is supported by SLA research and helps us define authentic experiences. Tasks, such as completing a transaction at the bank on the first day of a study abroad program, are derived from goals that, broadly stated, might be used to develop linguistic competence, perhaps focusing on accuracy, fluency, or complexity (Skehan, 1998), or, similarly, to develop sociolinguistic, intercultural, or pragmatic competence.

Unfortunately, although the definition of task has shifted over time to be more learner centered (Mishan, 2004), in most L2 classroom practice, learners are often unaware of the goals of a particular task, nor do they have much agency in choosing which tasks to complete. Therefore, the primary perspective of TBLT has remained psycholinguistic in nature, whereby much of the focus is on the task itself. In spite of good intentions, instructors often forget that the goal of the task is supposed to be the learner's goal, rather than just a feature of the task that matches the performance objective. For example, the task may originally be designed by the instructor to cover two primary functions, such as asking questions about cashing a traveler's check and asking for directions to the nearest ATM. Although the learners may share the desire to conduct business in a bank by asking the right questions and getting the services they need, learning to figure out how to cash a traveler's check and asking directions may not match the learner's intention, especially now that traveler's checks are rarely used and GPS units and smart phones easily direct people to specific places. In view of this conundrum, many have called for awareness instruction (Nunan, 2004) and more focus on learning strategies (Oxford, 2006); in some process-oriented approaches (Breen & Candlin, 1980; Ellis, 2003), learners are given more control over task choice and goal setting. Still, the disconnect between learner-driven and curriculum-driven goal orientation remains, in our opinion, the biggest challenge of making *task* a useful concept for the practice of L2TL. Digital game practices, including the design of and participation in game activities, offer a means to address this challenge and create inherently learner-centered experiences.

2.2.2 Your reflections

1. Consider the defining elements of an L2 learning task—primary focus on meaning; authentic, real-world use; goal orientation; and assessment of task outcome. Why are these important? Are there other elements you would add to the list? Elements you would take away?
2. Think of an L2 learning task you recall doing as a learner. Did it fit the definition of a task in this chapter? What was the goal? How aware of the goal were you at the time? How might this task differ from other language learning activities you did?
3. Think of an L2 learning task you implemented as a teacher. Did it fit the definition of a task in this chapter? How aware were learners of the goal at the time? Do you agree that it is important for learners to be aware of the goal of a task? Why or why not?

2.3 CRITICISMS OF TASKS IN L2TL

The use of tasks in L2TL has been critiqued on a number of accounts. Common criticisms include the following:

- Learners do not always share the goal of the task with the task designer, the instructor, the curriculum, or even other students, resulting in an outcome that may not accurately reflect what the learner learned from it.
- An authentic task does not guarantee that a learner has an authentic or meaningful experience with it.
- TBLT, at least in its strong form, is more learning driven than learner driven.

We are not the first to make these points, but we do hope to show them in a new light informed by insights from digital games and their associated behaviors. In the following section, we discuss each criticism in more detail.

2.3.1 Same task, different activities

Researchers (e.g., Breen, 1987; Ellis, 2003) have noted a fundamental problem between the intended task and actual learner activity in TBLT. As noted by Kumaravadivelu (1991, p. 100), "it is almost inevitable that there will be a mismatch between teacher intention and learner interpretation" of a given task. For example, among other causes, a mismatch might be cultural, whereby the learner does not have the cultural background knowledge to complete a task. The mismatch may be attitudinal, whereby the learners do not accept as a legitimate means of learning the role-playing or suspension of disbelief required by some tasks. Kumaravadivelu calls for research into "learners' personal reasons and concepts" (p. 107) for interpreting tasks in particular ways. We agree with those TBLT researchers who advocate awareness and learning strategy approaches that promote learner autonomy. In this way, it is not just teachers and researchers, but also the L2 learners themselves, who understand the nature of possible mismatches. Learners are active participants in aligning the tasks with overarching language learning goals.

The goal (i.e., the "what" of the activity) and the operation (i.e., the "how" of the activity) may appear to be quite similar across learners at first; however, because the motives are different, the same task is a different activity for different actors. Just as a movie theatre full of viewers does not experience the same movie in the same way, each learner experiences tasks and other elements in the classroom uniquely. Cultural-historical activity theory (CHAT) (Lantolf, 2000; Lantolf & Appel, 1994; Lantolf & Thorne, 2006; Leontiev, 1978) contributes to this discussion from a theoretical perspective, emphasizing the differences between *task* and *activity*. Just because people are doing the same action, or task, does not mean that they are doing the same activity, because of differing motives (Coughlan & Duff, 1994). Not surprisingly, all human activity is mediated by artifacts, whether language, experience, or tools such as tasks. Each individual brings varying motives, which are usually socially constructed, to a particular activity. Key to overcoming this disconnect in the classroom is recognizing the distinction and placing special emphasis on both task and activity to provide positive experiences for language learners. Acknowledging this is especially important in assessment. If learners' interpretations of a task do not align with those of the instructor and curriculum, the outcome may not accurately reflect what the learner is actually learning and may be counterproductive for future experiences.

These considerations underscore the necessity for acknowledging differing motives and integrating learner-driven elements into the design of L2TL curricula, game mediated or not. It is important to allow learners choice in defining goals to include their motives and to align instruction-driven goals to include learner agency. Teaching learners to be aware of their own motives and enabling them to drive instruction through learner agency and productive instructor-learner communication may accomplish this alignment. Although we cannot provide one-on-one instruction to every learner, we can increase learner choice in order to allow for a variety of experiences. Games, as we discuss later, are structured on the very notion of player-driven choice, so that players are always aware of what they are doing and why—without this agency, players will quickly lose motivation to continue playing.

2.3.2 Authentic tasks are not always authenticated

Authenticity is a buzzword often utilized in relation to both language and task and, as mentioned earlier, is a critical consideration in task design. Ultimately, it is the experience of the learner that creates authenticity, and, therefore, the focus should remain on the experience, as opposed to only on materials them-selves (Cook, 2000; Widdowson, 1978; van Lier, 2004). In considering TBLT, it is important to not only create tasks that are authentic and relevant, but also to give in-depth consideration to the various experiences learners have with those tasks. This could involve, for example, giving learners a variety of tasks from which to choose and providing flexible assessment measures that evaluate each individual learner's experience. Cook (2000) also notes that this authen-tic experience may be had when playing with form as well as when working with meaning. He adds that L2 materials and syllabi unnecessarily avoid con-troversial topics (e.g., intimacy and conflict), which many students may find meaningful and authentic.

Language play, a concept first explored in Chapter 1, adds further insight to our understanding of task. Cook (2000) challenges many of the tenets of communicative TBLT. These entail, for example, the assumption that learning correlates with work, whereas play does not, or that repetition to mastery, a tool that games count on extensively, is not a worthwhile learning technique. We align with Cook's call for focus on the playful, ludic function of language in L2TL. A game-mediated L2 learning activity can incorporate a ludic focus as easily as a focus on interpersonal expression or on the negotiation of ide-ational meaning. As we explore in detail in Section 2.4, digital games provide a variety of means for creating, and engaging with, these authentic experiences. However, it is important to keep in mind that learners may reject a genuine game as an L2 learning tool and may have trouble authenticating their experi-ence with it, just as they may have a meaningful experience playing an invented activity in a game-based synthetic L2 immersion environment. Although cultur-ally and linguistically genuine materials are ideal, it is learner engagement with them that makes them authentic. The issue comes down to learner awareness of a task goal, as well as agency in choosing to engage in the task, regardless of whether or not the task is traditional or game mediated.

2.3.3 Privileging instruction-driven over learner-driven design

As mentioned previously, strong versions of TBLT are driven by the belief that L2 pedagogy should derive from the findings of sound SLA research. For example, two-way information gap tasks (e.g., jigsaws) are touted as the ideal task design for negotiation of meaning leading to attention to form (Pica, Kanagy, & Falodun, 1993). Changing the parameters of a task, for example, the extent to which it affords a convergent or divergent outcome, will lead to different amounts and qualities of interaction. In this way, tasks are ontologically **learning driven**, rather than **learner driven**. Furthermore, the pressures that institutions be accountable for their students' learning have led to task goals being defined as assessment objectives, rather than as objects of learner-driven activity. This assessment-driven focus, we believe, can disenfranchise learners from their own learning.

Although we agree that the design of learning environments should reflect a sound understanding of learning principles, we believe that sole reliance on a learning-driven approach makes it too easy to put learners into the role of passive recipients, whereby learning happens because of some internal processes at least partially beyond their control or because they will be tested on it. When learning is construed this way, learner agency becomes something of an afterthought. This shortcoming has been addressed by calls for learner-centered amendments to TBLT (e.g., Breen, 1997; Nunan, 2004; Van den Branden, 2006). As a caveat, we also caution against thinking of "learner driven" as a simple solution, because learners do not always know what they need or want. Moreover, some learners have, unfortunately, come to view themselves as passive recipients of learning, and that assessment is what counts. We advocate, instead, striking a balance between learner-driven and instruction-driven uses of tasks, whereby "instruction" is an amalgam of learning-, instructor-, curriculum-, and assessment-driven needs. This approach puts the learner on equal ground with the instruction.

For insight, we turn to digital gaming. Digital games are not entirely open ended and player driven, but players are still provided enough agency (or sometimes merely the illusion of agency), so that they are in the driver's seat and know what, how, and to where they are driving. A game that does not provide its players a sense of agency quickly loses its market, because no one will play it. When a player does not know the object of the game, it can be argued that the player technically is not even playing the game. To draw a parallel, L2 learning tasks with which the learners have no agency in what they are learning are implemented all the time; yet people will argue that they can predict and assess what is being learned. Although we do not claim that digital games are a panacea to the problems of tasks in L2TL, they have developed over the past several decades into highly motivating, complex learning environments that deserve attention as we work toward the continued improvement of L2TL.

2.3.4 Your reflections

1. Have you had experiences teaching (or learning) an L2 in which your learners (or you) got something out of a task that was not the intended objective? Was what the students (or you) learned worthwhile?
2. What is the value of genuine language and materials in the L2 classroom? Do you agree that students can have authentic experiences with artificial materials?
3. To what extent do you think the L2 task and curriculum design processes are learning, assessment, or learner driven? What are the benefits and drawbacks of having these aspects drive the design process?

2.4 GAME PLAYING AS *GOAL-ORIENTING* BEHAVIOR

In this section, we turn our attention to the basics of game design and the experience of gameplay, for which goal orientation is at the heart of game-mediated activity. Although L2TL is not the focus of this section, we encourage you to return to the issues previously presented in this chapter to make connections and draw game-informed insights.

2.4.1 How is game playing goal oriented?

A game usually has a single overarching goal or **object of the game**—what one has to do successfully to win it. For example, one might have to save the princess (*SuperMario Brothers*) or reach the highest level of gameplay to become part of an elite group of gameplayers (*World of Warcraft*). At the same time, a game is an organized collection of interrelated tasks, each one being a group of "interesting choices" (Meier, 2003, as cited in Juul, 2005)[1]. Each task offers an objective, with the implication that the player has, or can develop, the skills necessary to reach it. These can be, for example, physical skills, such as jumping or hiding, and/or mental skills, such as puzzle solving and searching. There are usually multiple tasks to choose from, except in tutorials and early sheltered levels, when only one or very few choices are offered, with the understanding that this scaffolding is necessary to develop the skills needed for gameplay. In this way, a well-designed game is goal oriented; it aligns player-driven goals with game-driven goals by scaffolding gameplay and offering players choices, which imparts player agency. Goal orientation becomes a dynamic, negotiated, and continuous process, better understood as **goal orienting**, as a player constantly reassesses abilities, risks, challenges, and rewards while playing.

When confronted with multiple tasks to choose from, players may first eliminate the tasks whose objectives do not align with their goals, and then, from among the remaining options, choose the tasks whose objectives they think they have the abilities to accomplish. For example, in *Treasures of Mystery Island* (see Figure 2.1), players are given task options in their notebook, which not only highlight the quests, but also gives hints and a backstory as needed.

Task choice requires the ability to assess the risk of the challenge and the value of the reward, which might be experience points leading to new and greater challenges or new resources for use in future challenges.[2] Additionally, in multiplayer gameplay, a player selects his or her goal while also considering the other players' goals and abilities. In many MMOGs, teams of players must align their abilities to accomplish difficult tasks. For example, in *Runescape*, players have the option to group in clans with shared resources to play the game together and, at times, complete clan-specific activities. A successful group requires players with different combinations of the 25 possible skills that can be developed through gameplay. As can be seen in Figure 2.2, these skills include combat (e.g., agility, fletching, hunter), survival (e.g., fishing, farming), and healing skills (e.g., herblore, magic, prayer). A variety of tasks can help further a player's abilities. As seen here, agility can be improved by completing the agility courses throughout the realm as well as by using different equipment.

---

[1]Whether these activities are technically tasks, with all the work-associated baggage that term carries, becomes a difficult question when one considers that players actively and voluntarily make these choices. Still, for lack of a better term, we use *task* here for a bounded, in-game, goal-oriented activity.

[2]This feedback system is both simple and complex and is what drives gameplay operationally. See Chapter 4 for more information.

FIGURE 2.1 Treasures of Mystery Island (Spanish version) *Source*: Alawar Entertainment, Inc. (2012).

FIGURE 2.2 Runescape *Source*: Jagex Games (2001).

Group cooperation requires constant analysis, renegotiation of various demands, and communication among players, which can often result in additional authentic language experiences for learners (for further discussion, see Bryant, 2006; Thorne, 2003; Thorne, Black, & Sykes, 2010).

Even after goal orienting with all this in mind, the player often has several objectives operating at once, originating in multiple tasks that are layered and interwoven, sometimes overlapping and sometimes conflicting. Successfully reaching them may require various combinations of strategy, logic, deduction, and dexterity, usually in conflict with elements of chance (Fullerton, 2008). It should also be noted that games offer only as many options as a player can face at once. Having limited choices, the player is still able to make reasonable choices, maintaining his or her sense of agency. At the same time, the player does not become overwhelmed by an infinite number of possibilities, making gameplay prohibitively complex or difficult. A mismatched or unbalanced play experience, in the form of too many or too few options or too many challenges of the same type may lead a player to give up and choose not to play. If the tasks are too easy, the player gets bored and loses interest; if they are too hard, the player becomes frustrated and ultimately gives up. As has been pointed out by emerging research in digital games and L2TL (e.g., Purushotma, Thorne, & Wheatley, 2008; Sykes, Reinhardt, & Thorne, 2010) this varied, scaffolded, and player-driven game mechanism helps practitioners overcome many of the criticisms of tasks discussed in this chapter, for example, the lack of learner agency and task authenticity.

2.4.2 How are game tasks designed?

Tasks are organized differently in different games, and some games offer more choices and customizability than others. There are many kinds of in-game tasks, and although most games offer a variety, certain genres usually focus on particular types of tasks. Fullerton (2008) offers a taxonomy that illustrates the variety of objectives and task types a game might have (Table 2.1). Exploring this variety in light of L2TL can expand the repertoire of possible in-class task types, as well as offer some insight into how a variety of tasks types can be employed simultaneously for different learning needs and purposes.[3]

Some games are designed like theme parks (Aarseth, 2003), where players can choose tasks depending on their personal goals and playing style, often in differently themed areas. Others offer a sandbox, where the players can invent their own goals and play the game for purposes not necessarily intended by the designers; many simulation and management games, for example, are purposefully designed this way. This **open-ended design** is understood as a collection of rules that results in **emergent play** (Juul, 2005), as opposed to a **progression design**, common to adventure games and interactive fiction, which results in more predictable, **linear play**. Many of the most successful games are hybrids of both styles or offer various designs in a single game to appeal to different player styles.

In some games, particularly adventure and role-play games such as MMOGs, a collection of smaller tasks is called a quest, for which there is one large reward for completion. The various tasks offered in a game may be core or

---

[3]For more on game genres, see Appendix II: Guide to Game Types and Genres.

Table 2.1 Objectives and task types

Category	Objective	Sample Task Types	Common Genres
Capture	take or capture something	• find a key that will open a door • capture enemy territory	adventure, action, roleplay, strategy
Chase	catch something, or avoid being caught	• run through a maze • follow a trace left by a captive	adventure, action, roleplay
Race	reach a goal in a particular time	• finish cooking a dish in time • drive to the finish line before a competitor	adventure, action, roleplay, simulation management, strategy
Rescue/Escape	lead something or somebody to safety	• enter a cave, release a prisoner, and escort the prisoner back to his or her home	adventure, action, roleplay, strategy
Alignment	arrange or align elements	• put the parts of a secret message in order • get 5 Xs in a row	adventure, simulation management, strategy
Forbidden Act	avoid a particular activity	• avoid choosing the curtain hiding the goat	adventure, action
Construction	build, collect, maintain, or manage objects	• create a successful farm • sew a jeweled vest	roleplay, simulation management, strategy
Exploration	explore a given area	• find the capital of a new territory • see the breeding grounds of a rare butterfly	adventure, roleplay, strategy
Solution	solve a problem or puzzle	• translate the secret code • complete the crossword	adventure, strategy
Outwit	gain and use knowledge in a particular way	• use the invisibility elixir at the right moment and avoid detection	adventure, roleplay, simulation management, strategy

Source: Adapted from Fullerton (2008).

tangential to completion of a quest, and players are often given several choices of tasks within a quest. For example, in an adventure game, it may be necessary to open a door to get to the next room, but first, the key must be found, but a watchdog guards it. Alternatively, one can collect all the alchemical ingredients required to create a key, or distract the dog with a bone that was found earlier, or wait until the full moon, when the door will magically be unlocked. In any case, it is up to the player to decide, and there are often several optimal choices, depending on the player's goal and the skills and resources the player has at his or her disposal.

In-game tasks can involve both **spatial** and **temporal elements**. Spatially, a game may be divided into rooms, buildings, cities, lands, or areas. Temporally, a game may have an introduction, a tutorial, and cut scenes. A game usually has a narrative introduction contextualizing the game narrative and presenting the goal or object of the game. A tutorial typically introduces the primary game rules and tasks. Some games have **cut scenes**, which are narratives that run independent of the gameplay, such as small video clips between or embedded in game tasks. Nearly all games have **levels**, which are temporally bounded in that a player has to finish certain tasks and gain enough experience to level up, or move to a higher level. Levels are also spatially bounded in that players may be restricted to a particular area of the game until they have leveled up.

2.4.3 Your reflections

1. How is the process of goal orienting in gameplay similar to using language in an L2 learning task?
2. Look at the tasks in Table 2.1. Which may have parallels in traditional L2 learning tasks? Which do not and, if not, how might they be integrated in L2TL? What kinds of language may emerge from these more nontraditional, gamelike tasks?
3. What parallels do you see in the idea of game-as-theme-park or game-as-sandbox and the design of L2 learning tasks and environments?
4. How could in-game quests be used as L2 learning tasks? What spatial and temporal elements could translate into L2 learning tasks?

2.5 SUMMARY AND IMPLICATIONS

The following points summarize the main ideas of this chapter on goals, with implications for game-informed L2TL:

1. Digital games share goal orientation as a design feature with L2 learning tasks, but game tasks are fundamentally player driven, whereas L2 learning task design is sometimes learner driven, but often driven primarily by agents other than the learner. Drawing on lessons learned from digital games affords additional possibilities for creating learner-driven experiences.
2. Digital games show us that goal orientation is itself a dynamic, continually negotiated, and ongoing activity, better understood as goal orienting, rather than a static quality or essentialized trait.
3. Digital game–mediated L2TL fits with a balanced task-based approach, whereby learning emerges from the interaction of learner-driven and instruction-driven goal-orienting activity. Although instruction is necessarily informed by the instructor, learning research, assessment demands, and curriculum mandates, it is less effective in implementation if learners have no agency.
4. From a goals perspective, a digital game should be evaluated based on what the players are asked to do in the game, and whether that can be integrated with instruction-driven demands without sacrificing the player-driven quality of the in-game task objectives.

5. Genuine digital games and constructed synthetic immersive environments are useful for L2TL in different ways, the former as cultural products and processes, and the latter as customizable learning environments. Authenticity is a matter of learner-player experience, rather than a quality inherent to the material itself.
6. Many in-game tasks are not real world but are authenticated because they offer real choice to a player, even if the game designer predetermines those choices. In addition, they offer ways of using language that are outside the traditional scope of language classrooms.
7. Digital games are designed in ways that have parallels in L2TL, and certain design elements, for example, play styles, quests, and various spatial and temporal elements, can be adapted for use in L2TL (Purushotma et al., 2008).

2.6 A GAME-ENHANCED SCENARIO: *THE MUSEUM GAME*

In consideration of the insights discussed in this chapter, we return to our learning scenario using a game-enhanced L2TL approach.

Profesor Martín has researched and evaluated several low-cost casual adventure games for his intermediate Spanish class. He has found one that is thematically about a series of art thefts at a string of museums (*Art Thief*, http://www. agame.com/game/art-thief.html). Based on the game's reusability, four copies are purchased and are loaded on four language lab computers. As a lab activity the next day, he goes through the tutorial of one of the games for 10 minutes with his students and explains that each of them should play the game for at least one hour during open lab time as homework over the next week. He then asks them to complete a written journal task in which they describe their experience playing the game from the perspective of the game protagonist, a detective attempting to determine who is committing the crimes. In class a few days later, as a second task, Profesor Martín introduces a news report reading and discussion activity about the actual theft of a famous painting in a Spanish museum and has students write, as homework, their reaction to the painting and the burglary, and they speculate who could have stolen the painting. He then asks the students, in groups, to discuss their opinions of the actual art theft while referring to their reaction papers. Finally, when the first game journal activity is due, the groups are asked to write and perform a skit for a new level for the game in which the imaginary detective must find the painting that has been stolen. The class then engages in a critical discussion task on the similarities and differences among the game, the imaginary dialogues and game levels, and the real art theft.

Erica, Mateo, Lillian, and Roland are excited about the class and believe they might be learning something. In addition, the activities are fairly difficult. Erica had trouble getting access to the lab when she needed it but eventually was able to complete her required game time and actually enjoyed finding the missing art. Mateo, on the other hand, was at first not excited at all and said he thought the idea of playing computer games was not appropriate for the hard work of learning Spanish. However, upon completion of the full unit, he felt like he had learned something and really enjoyed comparing the real news report with the fictional game. Lillian and Roland found that their experiences playing the game any way they chose afforded them a sense of agency and autonomy. Lillian focused on finding as much art as possible, and Roland focused on learning as much about the in-game characters as possible. Also, despite their seemingly different gameplay experiences, documenting their gameplay from the perspective of the protagonist forced them to focus on the language of the game, which was all about art museums and crime solving. In the dialogue activity, most groups took on a playful stance, presenting situations in which the detective, classmates, the King of Spain, and Profesor Martín himself committed the art thefts in the game. In their game journal papers, students used many new vocabulary items introduced by the game, which also helped them read the actual news report and write and discuss their reactions to it. Language from both the journal and report activity were then recycled in the dialogue and critical discussion activities, but in transformed registers. Profesor Martín was pleased by the outcome of the week's instructional module.

2.6.1 Scenario questions

1. What is your reaction to the game-enhanced scenario? Taking a game-enhanced perspective, how might it have been better, or how could it have been worse?
2. What were the four tasks and their instructional objectives? How did the instructor incorporate elements of learner choice and agency in them? How did he combine curriculum needs with learner-driven goal orienting in the game?
3. What was the role of the game in the other classroom tasks (e.g., the news report)? How did the instructor complement the in-game tasks the students completed with the journaling and dialogue tasks?
4. How did different learners authenticate the tasks differently?
5. If you know Spanish, how do you think the activities might have encouraged the use of the subjunctive voice and target vocabulary?

In this scenario, Profesor Martín uses a literacy-informed, integrated approach. He creates a set of game-enhanced learning tasks whereby learners achieve curriculum goals in learner-driven and authentic or, rather, authenticated ways. The tasks are not game driven, but are driven by the activity of the learner-players, in balance with instructional demands. Learners are given options and the means to develop awareness and autonomy. In gameplay, the language is both a means and an input object—learner-players are using the L2 as the linguistic means of gameplay and the fictional content of the game serves as linguistic input. At the same time, the tasks incorporate multiple sources of input and multiple forms of output. At another level still, the learners are asked to transform their experiences into other modes, for other functions, that is, other genres such as conversations and opinions, and to develop critical awareness of digital gaming. A literacy-informed approach is only one approach to game-enhanced L2 pedagogy—in coming chapters, we will explore other approaches through different scenarios.

2.7 GAME-MEDIATED APPLICATIONS

In this section, we offer three applications of some of the concepts discussed in this chapter. Each is derived as a specific example of the general implementation frameworks we presented in the introductory chapter of this book. We first offer a description of the game-enhanced, game-journaling activity envisioned in the scenario. We follow this with a framework for designing tasks and goals in a game-based L2 learning environment, and then we offer final questions and ideas for game-informed reflections.

2.7.1 A game-enhanced L2 writing activity: Game journaling

The objective of this activity is for L2 learner-players to develop awareness of how playing a digital game is a goal-oriented activity that involves choice. The activity has two parts: (1) a tutorial task in which the instructor introduces the game by demonstrating the tutorial and having the students go through it in pairs or groups and (2) the journaling task that students complete on their own, by filling out a chart that explains what they did in the game and what their goals were while playing it. The purpose of the tutorial task is to prepare students for the journaling task.

Procedures

1. Choose a game for the learners to play—if necessary, use Appendix II: Guide to Game Types and Genres and the framework outlined in Appendix III: Evaluating Digital Games for L2TL. If the game is not browser based, have it installed on the computers that you will use to demonstrate, and on those that the students will use to play the game. Spend some time playing the game yourself and imagining the demonstration and activity. Customize the activities as needed.
2. Introduce the activity to the class and distribute the activity sheets (e.g., 2A and 2B below). Make sure learners know the objectives and expected outcome of the tasks. You can also have them predict possible outcomes other than those originally intended.
3. Use a computer with a projector to demonstrate the game. For the demonstration, go through at least part of the tutorial or basic gameplay tasks, checking for comprehension and understanding. If possible, ask students to direct you and make individual choices for you as you play.
4. Have students complete the tutorial in pairs or in small groups, and complete Activity 2A: Tutorial Task. If the game is particularly complex, you may want to prepare questions ahead of time to check their understanding of the important gameplay rules as they are playing it. Alternatively, you could ask them to get to a certain point in the game tutorial, indicating they reached the target.
5. At the end of the session, go over their answers in class, and if desired, collect Activity 2A for assessment.
6. Go over the journaling task with students.

Notes

- The task can be customized for class needs; for example, another row could be added to Activity 2B where students note particular vocabulary or language points. For more advanced students, more prose might be required.
- The number of entries should be predefined; for example, each student might be required to play the game and complete an entry in the journal afterward at least three times.
- It may be useful to provide a sample entry for students, customized for your game. Also, the activity could be done in subsequent lab sessions in pairs or groups, instead of as homework.
- The completed journals can be used for subsequent, related tasks, for example, a conversation activity in which students share their journals in pairs or groups or an extension activity in which students write longer descriptions of their gameplay experiences in other genres.

2.7.2 Designing a game-based L2TL environment: Focus on goals

The prospect of designing a game-based L2 teaching and learning environment can be overwhelming, but also powerful and engaging. Because of this complexity, each chapter in this volume is focused on a specific game element. Chapters can be used independently or in conjunction with the game-based activities from the other chapters. In this section, we offer a framework that both instructor-designers and L2 learners can use to think specifically about tasks and goals in the design of game-based L2TL environments (i.e., a synthetic immersive environment). For learners, the activity builds game literacy, language awareness, and strategies that promote learner autonomy. Depending on the level of instruction, the whole activity can be completed in the target language or specific elements can be designated target language only.

ACTIVITY 2A

Learning the tutorial

Answer the following questions after playing the game tutorial with your partner.

Name:

1. Explain what you initially like about the game and what you dislike about it. Make sure you provide reasons.
2. Name three different tasks you can do in the game.
3. For each task, explain *why* you need to do it to play the game.
4. Write four words and two phrases you needed to know to complete the tasks.

ACTIVITY 2B

Game journal (with a sample entry completed in italics)

Fill out the information in the columns about your game experiences. You should have at least three entries by the due date.

Name: *Erica*
Game: *A Castle in Time*

Entry	1	2	3
Date and amount of time spent playing.	*Nov 11, 10 min.*		
What did you do in the game?	*I searched the beach for treasure chests.*		
Describe one task you did.	*I used a shovel to dig up the chests.*		
Explain why you did it.	*Some of the treasure chests contained keys to unlock the castle gate.*		
Explain what you will do the next time you play.	*I want to find the princess in the courtyard.*		
What new strategies did you learn about the game?	*If you use a magic shovel, it takes less time to dig.*		
Something you liked or disliked.	*I thought the throne room was really beautiful, but I got annoyed at the music.*		

Procedures

1. Prepare, modify, and translate the activity sheet as necessary.
2. In class, explain to the students that they will help design a digital game that will help teach the target language. Explain the goal of the activity—to help them practice the language, develop critical awareness about games, and imagine a fun and effective way to learn.
3. Have the class first brainstorm names of popular digital games that they play and write them on the board.
4. With your help (and the help of Appendix II: Guide to Game Types and Genres if necessary), have the students identify the genres and types of the games they've brainstormed, specifically focusing on the tasks within those games.

CHAPTER 2 Game design activity: Design a digital game to learn [insert language]—Focus on goals

You have been given a grant to help build a digital game that will help students learn [insert language]. One step in the design process is coming up with the types of tasks and goals the game will have. As a group, design the goals of your game by answering the following questions. Be sure to include as much detail as possible.

1. Basic Information
    a. What will you learn?
    b. What type of game is it (e.g., simulation, adventure)?
    c. What is the object of the game (what a player does to win)?
    d. What is the context of the game (setting, characters, etc.)?
2. Tasks
    a. What sorts of activities and tasks can a player do in your game?
    b. Choose one task and describe it by answering the following questions:
        i.   What is the task?
        ii. What is the object of the task?
        iii. What does the player have to do to complete the task?
        iv. Why would the player do the task?
        v.   What does the player need to do the task?
        vi. What else can the player do instead of the task?
    c. What rewards does completing the task give the player?
    d. How are your tasks designed to help people learn [insert language]?
    e. Why do you think these tasks will be especially effective?
    f. Do you think players might do something different from what you intended? Why?
3. Storyboard: Create a storyboard in which you illustrate the experience the player has while doing one or more of the tasks you described.
4. Dialogue: Write a conversation between an in-game character and the player that focuses on the task you described.

5. Have groups choose a type of game and come up with a list of the tasks that players do in the game. If necessary, adapt and discuss Fullerton's (2008) objectives chart in Table 2.1.
6. Introduce the activity using the customized worksheet (see Chapter 2 game design activity).

2.7.3 Your game-informed reflections

A game-informed approach suggests a reconceptualization of task and goal orientation in the classroom. It is not embodied in one specific learning activity. Reflect on the chapter and write about and/or discuss the following topics:

1. Think about a particular class or course, and how students have responded to particular tasks. Based on the chapter discussions, how might you reconceptualize them? Are your tasks designed to promote learner agency

and choice throughout the learning process? If not, how could they be revised to encourage a learner-driven approach? Is there space for an authenticated learner experience?

2. Think of a traditional task that might be game enhanced. How could the game enhancement help focus learners on goal orienting?

3. What are some challenges in converging, or striking a balance between, learner-driven and instruction-driven goals? In what situations is it appropriate for instructional needs or demands to drive the task and determine its goal? How can learners be engaged in those situations?

4. Sometimes a game provides what seems like choice and agency to the player, but in fact the choices are predetermined, and one is clearly the better choice. Why would game designers build in this illusion of choice? What purpose could it serve? What might be an equivalent in L2TL?

5. Action research is critical to furthering our understanding of tasks and goals in digital games for language learning. What types of research projects related to the topics of this chapter would be most interesting to you? How would you investigate, for example, the effectiveness of different types of game-mediated tasks? The complexity of tasks? Student task design?

■ ■ ■ ■ ■ ■

Interaction
With, through, and about digital games

3.1 A SCENARIO: *GAMES ARE FOR LONERS . . . OR ARE THEY?*

A high school German instructor, Frau Berutti, has been reading about digital games for language learning and is considering their use in her class. She knows that most of her students love digital games—they write about them in their journals, and they have even asked her how to say words such as *newbie* and *owned* in German.[1] She is not sure if she can use digital games in class, however. When she brought the idea to an administrator, he brushed it off because he had heard news stories that presented video games as unhealthy and socially isolating. Also, he was not sure how Frau Berutti could fit digital games into the already full curriculum whose first priority was meeting all of the benchmarks of the national standards. He also talked about how morally corrupt he thought a particular auto theft game was, and he mentioned a study that claimed that American teens who played video games for more than 20 hours a week were more depressed than other teens. Frau Berutti's administrator planted some seeds of doubt in her mind, but she was not sure how to respond.

Frau Berutti, however, has seen her own children playing games and has a different view. Her kids interact with the stories in the games and through the games with their friends. They also seem to talk about the games, coming up with strategies and critiquing them all the time—as a matter of fact, that is all they seem to talk about sometimes. Her 10-year-old daughter seems especially taken with adventure games—her favorite at the moment involves a detective who travels through time to interpret mysterious objects found on a deserted island. The other day she dropped the word *artifact* casually in an argument with her brother. He is 14, and he seems to prefer role-playing games—he

---

[1]In gamer slang, *newbie* is a slightly derogatory term for new player, and someone who is *owned* has been resolutely defeated.

spends hours playing with his guild (i.e., an established group of players who regularly collaborate in the game) online, and he was a little down yesterday because he said he did not heal as well as he should have when his group went into a dungeon, although Frau Berutti was not sure what that meant. Because he had friended her on Facebook, she once went and looked at the profiles of his friends who were in his guild group. She found nothing that seemed particularly antisocial about their pictures or profiles. Her daughter's friends had been over several times to play a music game, and they all seemed to act like normal 10-year-olds while playing the game—laughing, socializing, and talking about the game all the while.

3.1.1 Scenario questions

1. What concerns do you have regarding the use of digital games in the foreign language classroom? What concerns do you think administrators, parents, and community members might have?
2. Some people argue that games are addictive because they are more immersive than other forms of media. Do you agree? Why or why not?
3. Some believe that games are socially isolating. Do you agree? Why or why not?
4. Do you play games or know someone who does? For what purposes do game players (i.e., gamers) use language? How do gamers talk about games with one another?

This scenario presents a situation that educators, parents, and administrators may face when considering the use of digital games in the classroom. The debate regarding video games, violence, and antisocial behavior has strong support on both sides and is not the focus here. In our view, the criticism that digital games cause antisocial behavior because they are violent, addictive, and socially isolating is a chicken-and-egg argument: Are some people sociopathic because they play antisocial games, or do they play antisocial games because they are sociopathic? In either case, dismissing all games because of the violence of a few notorious ones or particular genres is like dismissing all cinema because there are horror, war, and pornographic movies. The thousands of games with nonviolent and sociable content do not make for exciting journalism and, in many cases, are ignored in the media. Moreover, we would like to challenge people to rethink the notion of video games being negatively addictive because of the societal stigma around their use. If people lose themselves in a book for hours, we do not say the book is addictive, but rather it is engrossing and well written. The same argument could be made for good games. In fact, Salen and Zimmerman (2004) highlight the need to make a clear distinction between the medical concept of addiction and a game that fully engages players. We challenge educators to consider this perspective. Finally, the argument that games are socially isolating ignores the fact that most multiplayer games are inherently social, and that most popular games have large communities of players whose core practices involve interactions with, through, and about games. These interactions emerge from the interactive qualities that designers build into games.

3.2 INTERACTION

L2TL and digital game design approach interaction in similar ways. In L2TL, theories from various perspectives consider interaction to be a central, if not the most crucial, aspect of L2 learning. Various approaches to L2TL include activities that promote interaction. Game studies theorists and game designers study how digital games can provide the potential for interaction, through interactive game design built around player choice and agency. The parallels are unmistakable, and they are the subject of this chapter. We first discuss research on interaction in L2 learning from a variety of theoretical perspectives. We then explore interaction in game-mediated L2 pedagogy with, through, and about games. We continue by presenting research on interactivity from a game studies/game design perspective, and by discussing several game-informed insights this research may provide. We conclude with a summary of the main points, a new teaching scenario, and ideas for teaching and research. Questions for discussion and reflection are included at the end of each major section.

3.2.1 Interaction in L2 learning

Interaction in L2 learning has been conceptualized in a number of ways. Perhaps the best-known approach is the *interaction hypothesis* (Gass, 1997; Long, 1983; 1996; Long & Robinson, 1998). Its main thesis is that interaction between learners and their environment is central to language learning, because this interaction provides opportunity for the **negotiation for meaning** (NfM). A learner is subjected to input and produces output based on comprehension of that input, which may result in feedback from an interlocutor. If there is a communication breakdown or misunderstanding, the subsequent NfM can lead to the learner noticing the particular formal qualities of his or her production (Swain, 1995) that led to the breakdown. Noticing is hypothesized to be a crucial aspect of acquisition (Schmidt, 1990). Some researchers have found evidence that certain kinds of classroom activities, such as jigsaw tasks, promote NfM more than other types of tasks (Pica, Kanagy, & Falodun, 1993). NfM can also occur in technology-mediated contexts such as chat (Pellettieri, 2000; Smith, 2003), and task type and learner status can impact the amount and type of NfM, just as in face-to-face contexts.

In contrast to mainstream interactionist frameworks, **socially informed** accounts of L2 learning, which include sociocultural theory, language socialization, and ecological perspectives, view interaction as a complex social phenomenon. From a socially informed view, language learning is sociocognitive in nature; that is, cognition cannot be considered separately from social interaction. L2 learning is inseparable from L2 use, and participation is the dominant metaphor (Lave & Wenger, 1991; Sfard, 1998). From a sociocultural theoretic view, meaning is not transmitted from one person to another, or negotiated only during communication breakdown; rather, it develops between users and is then internalized by the learner (Lantolf & Thorne, 2006; Vygotsky, 1978). Interaction is always mediated by symbolic artifacts, whether language, thought, or other resources such as technology. Language socialization researchers (e.g., Duff, 2012) see language use as a form of social practice. Learning is a matter of developing an identity recognizable to a community and practicing language appropriate to that identity (Lam, 2000). An ecological perspective (e.g., van Lier, 2004) acknowledges that interaction is a complex activity involving many factors, out of which meaning and, therefore, learning emerges. Ecological analysis considers all of the interrelationships among resources and potential interactions, or affordances, in a given learning context. From these socially informed perspectives, interaction is the means by which people co-construct meaning.

From a socially informed perspective, some interactionist tenets are inadequate (Block, 2003; Firth & Wagner, 1997). For example, the traditional NfM framework (Varonis & Gass, 1985) analyzes an interaction episode as consisting of the following phases:

1. A trigger, or the utterance that sparks nonunderstanding
2. An indicator, or the way the hearer shows that he or she does not understand
3. A response, or the way the interlocutor reacts, perhaps by restating or clarifying the original utterance
4. An optional reaction to the response by the hearer, showing new understanding

However, many times a hearer may misunderstand the message and continue as if he or she understands, or the hearer may understand the pragmatic intention of the message from context, even when it is otherwise incomprehensible. There may be issues of politeness and face at stake, because of the status or identities of those involved (Reinhardt, 2008). In other words, the traditional NfM framework may focus too narrowly on the ideational function of an interaction, whereas the interpersonal function is just as, if not more, important to comprehension.

A socially informed interpretation of interaction is informed by Halliday's (1978) functional perspective of language as a social semiotic (see Section 1.1), whereby all language has ideational, interpersonal, and textual meaning. In Halliday's view, an utterance has **ideational meaning**, referring to the basic semantic information being exchanged; **interpersonal meaning**, referring to the pragmatic qualities of the message; and **textual meaning**, or the discourse-level qualities of the message—that is, how it relates to other contexts. These correspond to the ideational *field* of the message, the interpersonal *tenor*, and the textual *mode*. L2 pedagogy theorist Kumaravadivelu (2006) argues that it is important to balance a focus on all three aspects in the L2 classroom. Traditional learning activities usually focus on the ideational field, or the basic semantic qualities of a message, not giving enough attention to the interpersonal tenor—that is, the sociopragmatic meaning of a message and the social relationship it indexes. Finally, attention to the mode of the interaction, or how the language relates to the context of situation and culture, is vital to learning (see Chapter 5). When L2 learning activities focusing on interaction do not give attention to all three levels, they may be only partially effective.

3.2.2 Your reflections

1. Consider the perspectives on interaction in L2TL described in this section, primarily interactionist and socially informed perspectives. In your opinion, what are the strengths and weaknesses of each perspective?
2. How is meaning simultaneously ideational, interpersonal, and textual? For example, consider the utterance "I won the game!" What does it mean at the ideational level? What interpersonal meanings might it have to the hearer? How might the meaning differ according to the contexts in which it is said?
3. What types of learning activities promote interaction on the various functional levels of meaning? How can the design of an activity encourage the negotiation or co-construction of meaning?

3.3 GAME-MEDIATED L2 INTERACTIONS

L2TL researchers have begun to examine game-mediated interactions in a variety of contexts—in and outside the classroom, single- and multiplayer games, vernacular and educational games, online and off-line. We believe that Halliday's and Kumaravadivelu's three-part understanding of language and L2 pedagogy provides a useful framework for understanding this research, and for conceptualizing interaction in game-mediated L2TL.

3.3.1 Ideational interactions *with* games

Several researchers have looked at how players might learn language with the simulation game *The Sims*. In this game, players develop simulated people, or avatars, and command them to do everything from working to eating to socializing. A player must know many vocabulary items to interact with the game, and playing the game helps the player learn them. Miller and Hegelheimer (2006) investigated the use of the game in an adult ESL classroom. They designed and implemented a series of supplementary materials for use with the game and found that learners who used the materials retained more vocabulary than those who did not. Their research suggests the importance of pedagogical mediation with the use of vernacular games and that, in some cases, simply playing a vernacular game does not guarantee learning the content. Purushotma (2005) reports on the development of an add-on program for *The Sims* that would let him easily look up translations for the German version of the game. He argues that the game's structure, in which the player does not just memorize vocabulary but has to use it in integrated meaningful goal-orienting activities, affords learning. He also shows that pedagogical mediation can be built into, or added onto games, which has implications for the design of game-based simulated immersive environments.

From our viewpoint, the meaning that is negotiated or co-constructed *with* games, that is, with the linguistic and cultural content of games, is primarily *ideational* in nature. The game designers determine the content, and the players learn it by interacting with the game. The ideational content of digital games, just as with the content of novels, movies, stories, or any other cultural product, benefits greatly when it is the objective of analytic learning activities, whether built into the game or through **wraparound activities** (i.e., activities related to gameplay that occur before, during, and after gameplay), that are explicitly designed to focus on linguistic and cultural content. During gameplay, many will experience this content and may subconsciously consider linguistic and cultural elements. However, the explicit addition of classroom activities to enhance the gameplay experience and focus learners' interaction with the game can have positive benefits. For example, the focus of the casual game *RU Emergency Response* (Figure 3.1), players must strategize to provide aid in global settings as members of an international relief agency. The quest in Figure 3.1 has players respond to an earthquake in Argentina. L2 learning wraparound activities could provide a structure for strategic group discussion about the task, focus on lexical and grammatical items related to the quest content, or ask learners to investigate actual earthquakes in Argentina or other areas. The scope and design of wraparound activities will always depend on learner needs and consideration of curricular demands.

3.3.2 Interpersonal interactions *through* and *around* games

Although thinking of games as useful based on their content has much potential, it is only one way of thinking about them. One danger in thinking of meaning as primarily ideational is that it leads to conceptualizing communication as

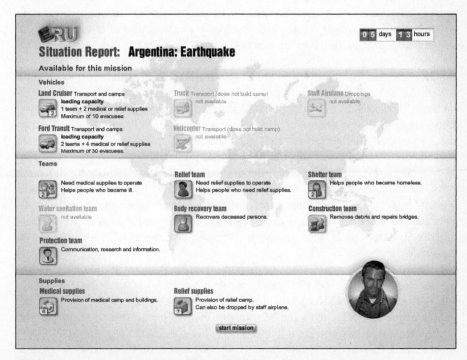

FIGURE 3.1 RU Emergency Response *Source*: Youda Games, Inc. (2008).

transmission and learning as reception, when learning is, in fact, much more. As discussed earlier, many L2TL researchers show us that learning is better understood as a matter of active negotiation or construction of meaning through social interaction. In other words, meaning is not only ideational, but also interpersonal. How you understand something depends not only on what is said, but who says it, and for what interpersonal reasons. In games, we can conceptualize that meaning is potentially co-constructed with other players or agents *through* or *around* games, rather than simply with the game content. These meanings emerge from the social activity of playing with others.

Many multiplayer online games allow players at a distance to communicate with one another through the game to complete joint activities such as trading and questing. Some games incorporate a chat tool whereby a player can read and participate in general chats with others playing the game in real time, carry on group chats with friends or teams, or engage in individual chats with one other player. Conversations can be directed at public activities such as trade, joint in-game tasks a gamer is doing with the other players, or general social topics. In some games, the interactions can even be role-played, whereby the players assume the voice of their avatars. Role-playing can lead to opportunities for exploration of new perspectives and identities (Lee & Hoadley, 2007).

L2TL researchers have noted that the variety of audiences and activities in multiplayer online digital games provides opportunities for linguistic and intercultural development. Thorne (2008) noted the transcultural, polylingual nature of interactions among players in *World of Warcraft*, and he analyzes online interactions between an American player and a Russian player. He showed that multiplayer online games can afford transcultural interactions and the development of polylingual identities, because they provide environments for social identity play. Zheng, Young, Wagner, and Brewer (2009) examined the English learning that took place in *Quest Atlantis*, a virtual world designed for educational purposes. They paired two teenage learners in China with similar native speakers in the United States and had them complete quests together. They showed that co-construction of intercultural understanding emerged in the game, and that different game quest-activity designs afforded different opportunities for negotiation. Piiranen-Marsh and Tainio (2009) observed two teens playing *Final Fantasy X*, an adventure/role-play game. Sharing the same physical space, the players interacted in their L1 and in their L2 English and voiced characters in the game via "other repetition." L2 learning emerged as one learner watched the other play, repeated the language used in voice-overs and by in-game characters, made plurilingual commentary, and engaged in language play.

If a vernacular game is multiplayer, game-enhanced L2 learning wraparound activities can be designed to promote social interaction by having students complete various game activities with other players as they play the game. In an MMOG, for example, players might be directed to team up and complete a wraparound activity as they play the game together. Similarly, game-based L2 learning environments should incorporate game designs that require learner-to-learner interaction through the game as an integrated element

FIGURE 3.2 Farm Frenzy 3 *Source*: Alawar Entertainment, Inc. (2011).

of gameplay. However, we do not believe this means that games that are not multiplayer are not useful for L2 learning. Supplemental wraparound classroom activities that promote learner-learner interaction can add an interpersonal element to single-player games, and students can be directed to play a single-player game in pairs, trios, groups, or even as a whole class. For example, if learners were playing *Farm Frenzy 3* as part of their Italian class, they could play in pairs and decide what to buy and sell at different times (Figure 3.2).

Although these activities are not part of the game per se, they play a critical role in encouraging social interaction and the co-construction of interpersonal meaning, in addition to ideational meaning. Well-designed wraparound learning activities should focus on the meanings embedded in the game, as well as on the meanings that emerge among players as they play.

3.3.3 Textual interactions *about* games

From an L2TL perspective, learning, whether inside or outside the classroom, is understood to take place in a larger context. Although different perspectives on L2TL research view the importance of context differently, everyone agrees that it plays a role. Language has meaning besides the ideational and interpersonal functions on a discourse or *textual* level (Halliday, 1978). For language learners, language is more easily understood when it is connected to larger situational and cultural contexts, making meaning more easily constructed. L2 teachers instinctively understand this, especially when practicing communicative language teaching. Even if students understand the ideational or interpersonal meaning of an L2 text, it becomes meaningful to them when it is connected to the immediate situation and, ultimately, to their daily lives and the world around them. In other words, unless it is *about* something they can relate to, meaning is difficult to construct.

This understanding has inspired some researchers to look at the L2 interactions that happen when learners make connections between previous experiences, the world around them, and the current situation. For example, Sykes and Holden (2011) created a mobile game for Spanish learning that students play by visiting various locations in the local community. The game requires that students interact with local linguistic and cultural content, including neighborhood Spanish speakers. The students reported a sense of meaningfulness from the activities, as they realized that what they learned in the classroom was about the local community. In another example, Lacasa, Martínez, and Méndez (2008) conducted a workshop in which the participants played a video game, *Tomb Raider*, and then created and performed a play using the game characters. Students also developed and posted a website discussing their critical experiences playing the game, focusing on the spatial architecture of the game world and the violent nature of many video games. Although the students were not L2 learners, the project showed that game-enhanced pedagogy could be highly effective when it is extended beyond the game and is connected to broader cultural discourses.

Game-mediated L2TL activities can and should connect the world inside the game with the world outside. Game-based applications can be created that have immediate and local relevance for learners. For game-enhanced learning, the many cultural, historical, and political discourses in vernacular games can be critically analyzed and discussed with learners. In addition, the cultural practices of game-playing communities can be used as learning resources. Although the content of some games may seem only tenuously related to a student's life outside the classroom, it is the connections between game discourses and personally relevant discourses that afford learning and make the language of interaction meaningful. It is the task of instructors and game designers to develop game-enhanced L2 learning wraparound activities and game-based L2 learning environments that afford meaningful interactions on ideational, interpersonal, and textual levels.

3.3.4 Your reflections

1. What sort of game-enhanced L2 learning wraparound activities could be created to preview, practice, or review the language found in a game task or quest? How can these activities promote ideational, interpersonal, and textual interaction?
2. Think of the notions and topics in a typical L2 curriculum. What sorts of games do you think might match various levels of language study? Refer to Appendix II: Guide to Game Types and Genres if necessary.

3. How might a game-based learning environment, created for L2TL, be designed to promote interaction on all three levels of meaning— ideational, interpersonal, and textual?

3.4 INTERACTION FROM A GAME DESIGN PERSPECTIVE

As we have seen, a socially informed perspective on L2TL (Halliday, 1978; Kumaravadivelu, 2006) offers a framework for thinking about interaction as ideational, interpersonal, and textual, which we connect to interaction with, through or around, and about games. In games studies, a similar parallel has been noted by Salen and Zimmerman (2004), who indicated that there can be (1) **formal interaction** with the game system itself, (2) **social interaction** with other players, or (3) **cultural interaction** with broader cultural discourses and communities. Game designers, however, understand that interaction is the outcome of interactive design, and that they can create only the conditions, or affordances, for interaction. They cannot control interaction completely; a player may choose at any time to not interact or to interact with the game in ways not anticipated by the designers or other players. This understanding, that interaction is contingent on player agency, offers insights for the design of game-mediated L2TL environments and can inform L2TL more broadly.

Games researchers (e.g., Juul, 2005; Salen & Zimmerman, 2004; Schell, 2008) note that interactivity is in many ways the defining element of digital games, separating them from other forms of media, such as books or films, that are not explicitly participatory. They note four types of interactivity—cognitive, functional, explicit, and cultural.

Cognitive interactivity happens in a player's mind, much like in the mind of a reader, music listener, or filmgoer. A cognitively interactive game draws players in, immersing them in a visual, auditory, narrative-rich, and even tactile experience. Like books, songs, or films, games incorporate text, visuals, sounds, narratives, and various themes, but unlike with those media, game designs must account for players being able to interact with those elements explicitly, possibly altering them.

Functional interactivity refers to the interface of a game and how it interacts physically with the player through the use of buttons, menus, and other tangible (or clickable) structures. Good interface design is extremely important to a game. It should be intuitive and ergonomic and become nearly invisible to players as they develop expertise. As we discuss further in Chapter 6, functional interactivity is essential for the attainment of player flow states while playing digital games.

Even though game designers have control over the functional interactivity of a game interface, it is more important for a player's sense of engagement that the **explicit interactivity** of the game is well designed. This third type of interactivity refers to structures designed into the game itself, not part of the interface, that are built around the concept of choice and decision making by the player. In a game, a player makes choices by choosing one action over another, sometimes with careful deliberation and sometimes in a split second. Salen and Zimmerman (2004) explained that these choices should have discernable and integrated consequences. In other words, players should be made aware through game feedback (see Chapter 4) how their in-game choices make a difference in the unfolding gameplay. This action-outcome relationship should not be tangential or inconsequential, but rather integrated into gameplay.

In some game genres, such as adventure or role-play games, designers can predetermine nearly every explicit choice a player will be able to make, because gameplay in those games follows a linear narrative pattern with a set number of storylines (for an L2TL application of this concept, see Neville, 2010). Designers have less control in action or strategy games, with which the gameplay experience emerges out of the combination of rule parameters (Juul, 2005), and the number of possible outcomes is exponentially larger. In multiplayer games, many in-game choices are designed to lead to player interaction. In this way, gameplay creates socially emergent behaviors and practices. Some designs promote collaboration, whereas others promote competition. For example, MMOG designers can promote collaboration by making some game activities, such as quests, more easily completed by groups of players than by solo players. Various game systems allow each player to develop unique skills that are potentially complementary to those of other players when they play in groups. Collaboration and competition can also be promoted by making certain useful resources in the game scarce and hard to win, but easy to share, trade, or sell. The combined effect of all these interactive choices is a sense of agency and engagement.

Finally, **cultural interactivity** refers to creation of and participation in **attendant discourses** around the game and the cultures and the communities that practice the particular game, as well as digital gaming more broadly. They may be very different from the cultures and discourses depicted by the game itself, which are placed there by the designers. Independent of designer control, communities grow around popular games, especially online multiplayer games, and players participate in a variety of communicative practices. Although players do gather in person, communities are primarily online in the form of discussion boards, resource wikis, and chat rooms, through which participants can exchange knowledge and advice and share **fan art** (i.e., art created from game content), **machinima** videos (i.e., animated features utilizing game assets), and **fan fiction** (i.e., narrative to extend or rewrite in-game narrative). Cognitive and explicit interactivity gives rise to cultural interactivity. For example, a game with complex narratives and highly artistic graphics may lead to new sociocultural practices in the form of online fan art and fiction communities. Other games have complicated rules that are the subject of discussion boards on which players discuss strategies, opinions, and political issues related to the gaming community. A popular multiplayer game may give rise to communities with unique interaction practices that are learned and negotiated both inside and outside the game.

3.4.1 Implications for L2TL

Game designers show us that interaction is a function of a good interactive design and that it can be promoted through immersive experiences, ergonomic interfaces, and discernable and integrated choices, as well as by connecting the game to the outside world. These principles are useful for the design of L2TL environments, whether or not game mediated, because they can promote ideational, interpersonal, and textual interactions. Experienced instructors know that an immersive learning environment is cognitively interactive and that it appeals to multiple senses, intelligences, and learning styles. Functionally well-designed and clear instructions for any learning activity are important, so that the time spent on learning how to complete an activity is minimized and the time spent actually doing the activity is maximized. Providing learners explicit choices in directing their own learning is crucial to the development of learner autonomy and a sense of agency (see also Chapter 2). Interaction can be promoted through judicious incorporation of collaborative, competitive, and distributive design principles, as any designer of an information gap or jigsaw learning task understands. Finally, as effective instructors know, it is vital to contextualize learning experiences and make connections between the culture of study and the students' world. Well-designed games show that context is key to learning—an idea we explore further in Chapter 5.

3.4.2 Your reflections

1. What aspect(s) of a traditional (i.e., not game mediated) L2 learning activity would correspond to cognitive interactivity as understood by game designers?
2. How do the directions or the logistics of implementing an L2 learning activity correspond to functional interactivity, and why are they important to an activity's success?
3. How is an L2 activity explicitly interactive, and why is it important for L2 learning?
4. What would it mean for an L2 learning activity to be culturally interactive, in the sense promoted by game designers? What sorts of activities are more or less culturally interactive?
5. When drawing on a game design perspective, are there additional implications for interaction in L2TL that are not mentioned here?

3.5 SUMMARY AND IMPLICATIONS

The following points summarize the main ideas of this chapter on interaction, with implications for transformed L2TL:

1. Interactionist research shows that in L2 interactions, *negotiation for meaning* may lead to L2 learning when learners notice differences. From a socially informed view, learning through interaction is highly contingent on social context.
2. Game-mediated L2 interaction can potentially be *with* the game content at the ideational level, *through* or *around* the game with other players at the interpersonal level, and *about* the game at the textual or discourse level.
3. L2 interaction *with* games can lead to the negotiation or co-construction of ideational meaning by focusing on linguistic and cultural content

embedded in the game. This content can correspond to the traditional topics of L2 curricula.

4. L2 interaction *through* or *around* games can lead to the negotiation or co-construction of interpersonal meaning with other players of the game during play, whether or not physically co-present.

5. L2 interaction *about* games can lead to the emergence of textual meaning by relating game playing to broader, more meaningful contexts, including personally relevant and cultural discourses.

6. Interactivity in digital games can be *cognitive, functional, explicit,* and *cultural.* These understandings can inform the design of L2TL environments, whether or not game mediated.

7. *Cognitively interactive* game design involves creating an immersive, multimodal gameplay experience with graphics, sounds, music, and narratives that engage players with the game. *Functional interactivity* is a matter of seamless, ergonomic, and nearly invisible interface design.

8. *Explicit interactivity* develops by offering players choices and decisions to make. If designed choices are not discernable and integrated, they do not lead to engagement. Explicitly interactive game designs afford social interaction by promoting collaboration and competition among players in various ways. *Cultural interactivity* involves attendant discourses and various social practices that emerge in player communities.

3.6 A GAME-ENHANCED SCENARIO: *SOCIAL INTERACTIONS AROUND SOCIAL NETWORKING GAMES*

In consideration of the insights discussed in this chapter, we return to our learning scenario using a game-enhanced L2TL approach:

After thinking about how her own children play video games, Frau Berutti has designed a few activities for her intermediate German students using the popular social networking game *Farmville*, which she has played herself for a few months. First, in the lab, she has her students set up Facebook to work with the social networking game being used. This includes giving students the choice to create new Facebook accounts or utilize the accounts they already have. In both scenarios, she asks them to set the interface language to German. She allows the students to develop identities that are similar to, or as different from, their real identities as they like. She presents basic computer use and social networking vocabulary in German, and she has them describe to one another how to do various Facebook tasks.

For the game-enhanced activity, she has students start playing the German version of Farmville and become one another's neighbors, which means they can visit others' farms and send and receive gifts. She introduces the game in the lab and has students who know the game try to explain to their classmates in German how to play it. She then has students play the game and tells them they need to reach level 5 in a week. After a week, she has the students complete a wraparound activity. Because Farmville includes much vocabulary about food and farming, she develops a *Jeopardy*-style quiz game whereby students guess the food item based on longer descriptions (e.g., "this vegetable is yellow and has small kernels"). For the answer, they have to search through the game to find the answers (in this case, "corn"). She then has small groups of students devise similar descriptions of vocabulary from the game, and she conducts an in-class quiz show using their descriptions. The students seem to enjoy the activity, and they ask for other activities using social networking games. They also begin to ask many questions about cultural elements in the game as well as pragmatic issues with some of the people they interact with in the game.

She goes to her administrator with an argument showing that game playing can in fact be highly social and that games can provide much productive, learning-focused interaction, especially when supplemented by wraparound activities. She explains her Farmville vocabulary activity, shows him the game in German, and presents some of the cultural information students have learned. He seems surprised and promises to reconsider his stance.

3.6.1 Scenario questions

1. Consider Farmville or another casual social networking game. If you are not familiar with one, we encourage you to play for 15–20 minutes in any language(s) of your choice. What sort of language is built into the game? How do players usually interact with, through/around, and about the game?
2. As you answer the following questions, consider the scenario just described. What tasks made up the scenario activity and what were their instructional objectives? How did the instructor incorporate interaction with, through/around, and about games in the tasks? How could she incorporate more interaction on other levels?
3. Into what traditional units or lessons could the content of a casual social networking game such as Farmville, focused on food and farming, fit? What other games have content that could fit with traditional curriculum topics? How could activities promote interaction with, through/around, and about the game?

3.7 GAME-MEDIATED APPLICATIONS

In this section, we offer three applications of some of the concepts discussed in this chapter. Each one is an example of the general implementation frameworks we presented in Chapter 1 of this book. We first offer a description of the game-enhanced interaction activity envisioned in the scenario. We follow with a framework for designing tasks and goals in a game-based L2 learning environment, and we then offer final questions and ideas for game-informed reflections.

3.7.1 Game-enhanced L2 speaking/listening activities: Game-mediated interactions

The objective of these activities is for L2 learners to develop awareness of how playing a digital game involves interaction on several levels: with, through/around, and about the game. Three different activities may involve the same or different games.

Procedures

1. For each activity, choose a game for the class to play—use Appendix II: Guide to Game Types and Genres and Appendix III: Guide to Evaluating Games if necessary. It may be the same or different games for each activity. If you use the same game, be sure the elements described here are included. Also, be sure to select and play the game in the target language.
   - For activity 3A, choose a game that incorporates dialogues between non-player characters, such as an adventure or role-play game.
   - For activity 3B, choose a multiplayer game that has an in-game chat function.
   - For activity 3C, have students choose a game that has an active community with online resources and fan websites. You may wish to find these online resources beforehand, if you think your students will not be able to find them on their own.
2. Spend some time playing the game yourself and reviewing the activity, translating and customizing the activity as needed.
3. Have students play the game and become familiar with it—in pairs/groups, in class, or on their own. This may take several hours of playtime.
4. Model the activity for the students and get them started on their own analysis.

Notes

- Activities may be customized so that students observe a particular kind of vocabulary, grammar, or culture point.
- Students may extend the activities with larger projects. For 3A, students may act out the interactions, compare game interactions with more authentic interactions, or write new interactions. For 3B, students may create a list of useful phrases for playing a game in the L2. For 3C, students may present the sites they have found or, within a site, their favorite gameplay tips, fan art, fiction, or videos.

ACTIVITY 3A

Interacting with games in the L2

For this activity, you should find an in-game character who interacts with you. Think about the conversation or interaction the character has with you.

1. How do you interact with this character? Is it written or vocal?
2. What is the character interacting with you about? Why is it important?
3. Choose a point where the character offers you a choice. What are your possible responses? How realistic are they? What other responses do you wish you could make?
4. Write out the interaction as a script.
5. Write down three new vocabulary or grammar items that you notice in the dialogue.

ACTIVITY 3B

Interacting through/around games

For this activity, you should notice the language you use with other people while playing the game. You should attempt to complete as many of the activities as possible in the target language. This language use can be through the in-game chat feature or around the game in person (e.g., working together to create a machinima video).

In-game chat option: Play the game for a while using the in-game chat function. Archive the chat transcript and open it for analysis.

Game talk option: Play the game in a group of two or three. While playing, the note taker should write down the language you are using to interact around the game, in your language or in the L2.

Look at the transcript or notes and answer the following questions:

1. What did you talk about?
2. Find a point where you talked about the game rules. What were you trying to figure out?
3. Find a point where you talked about the game design or stories in the game. What did you say?
4. What are some L2 phrases you might need to know to play the game in the L2 with other speakers?

ACTIVITY 3C

Interacting about games

For this activity, you should find an online resource that includes content for players of your game or one that has fan fiction, art, or videos related to your game. Browse the online space and answer the following questions:

1. Who develops and maintains the space?
2. What is the purpose of the space?
3. What language(s) is/are primary on the space? What are the secondary languages? Where are the users from?
4. Who uses the space?
5. How can users interact with each other in the space? What tools do they use?
6. What do users interact about? Give an example.
7. Find a useful playing tip, a fan fiction story, a piece of fan art, or a fan video, and evaluate it. What do you like or dislike about it?

3.7.2 Designing a game-based L2TL environment: Focus on interaction

As in previous chapters, this section focuses on the design of one specific element of the game, in this case, interaction. It should be used in conjunction with the content from the other sections on which you have worked (e.g., goals, feedback, and context). In this section, we offer a framework that designers, instructors, and learners can use to think about interaction in the design of game-based L2TL environments. Depending on the level of learner, the whole activity can be completed in the target language; alternatively, specific elements can be designated as target language only.

Procedures

1. Prepare, modify, and translate the activity sheet as necessary.
2. In class, explain to the students that they will be helping to design a digital game for language learning and will be focusing on interaction. This can be done in conjunction with the other design activities in other chapters or as its own process.
3. Explain the objectives of the activity—to develop critical awareness about games, to rethink interaction in language learning, and to design game interactions.
4. Have students complete the activities from Section 3.7.1 of this chapter so they have a better understanding of the nature of interaction and interactivity in games.
5. Have learners work in groups to complete the activity.

CHAPTER 3   Game design activity: Design a digital game to learn [insert language]—Focus on interaction

You have been given a grant to help build a digital game that helps students learn [insert language]. One step in the design process is imagining the interactions with, through/around, and about your game. As a group, imagine the interactions of your game by answering the following questions. Be sure to include as much detailed information as possible.

1. Basic Information
   a. What will you learn?
   b. What type of game is it (e.g., simulation, adventure)?
   c. What is the object of the game (what a player does to win)?
   d. What is the context of the game (setting, characters, etc.)?
2. Interactions
   a. **Formal interaction.** How will players interact with your game? How much comprehension (reading and listening) and production (writing, speaking, or making choices by clicking) will be involved? With what elements will players interact?
   b. **Social interaction.** How will players interact through your game with chat, or around your game when playing with friends or classmates? How will they use the L2 to do so?
   c. **Cultural interactions.** What out-of-game resources will you provide for players? How will you encourage players to create online resources and fan groups, if possible?

3. Screenshot: Draw a picture of the game interface to show how it supports interaction.
4. Dialogue: Write a branching conversation tree between a player and a non-player character in the game. Use a flow chart to indicate player options and the subsequent responses.

3.7.3 Your game-informed reflections

A game-informed approach suggests a reconceptualization of interaction in the classroom. It is not embodied in one specific learning activity. Reflect on the chapter and write about and/or discuss the following topics:

1. Think about an L2TL activity you have taught or done as a learner. What sorts of cognitive, social, and cultural interactions did the activity promote?
2. Think about the idea of functional interactivity in a non-game-mediated L2TL task or activity design. How does the interface of an L2TL activity, that is, the instructions and the process of learning how to do the activity, sometimes get in the way of actually doing the activity? How can the implementation of an activity become seamless, and how can this help learning?
3. Think about the idea of explicit interactivity in a non-game-mediated L2TL task or activity design. How would the outcome of an L2TL activity be discernable and integrated, and how important is it that the outcome is perceived this way by learners?
4. What is the place of collaboration and competition in the L2 classroom? What are the benefits and drawbacks of each one? How can they promote interaction? How can they lead to engagement in the learning process?
5. How could you incorporate game-informed notions of interaction and interactivity into your classroom, even without the use of digital games?
6. Action research is critical to furthering our understanding of interaction in digital games for language learning. What types of research projects would be most helpful? How could you investigate, for example, different kinds of game-mediated L2 interactions and how they relate to L2 learning?

Feedback

Real-time, individualized, and instructional

4.1 A SCENARIO: *THE FEEDBACK CHALLENGE*

Professoressa Feng

Professoressa Feng is in the process of grading her Italian class's exams for chapter 3. Although the scores are acceptable, she finds herself wishing for a more effective means to help students gauge their progress. In an ideal world, she would have time to give more detailed feedback to each student individually at various points throughout the course prior to the chapter exams. However, the reality of classroom, administrative, and service responsibilities makes it extremely challenging. Moreover, high-stakes assessments are a necessary component of her end-of-the-year report on learning outcomes. Professoressa Feng works hard to include formative assessment, that is, feedback meant to help improve performance. For example, she gives general suggestions for improvement after each communicative task, a weekly participation evaluation for each student, and personalized comments during pair and group work. These assessments are a consistent part of her everyday teaching practices, but there are 28 students in her class, making it difficult to address each student individually. She knows she cannot get to every student for every activity, so, in an effort to be thorough and careful, she systematically rotates among groups, giving feedback where she can. She mostly corrects grammar errors and answers questions about how to say certain words. Professoressa Feng then spends extensive time giving detailed, summative feedback on three formal writing assignments, four chapter exams, and one oral exam per semester. Despite her attention to student learning, the results are not exactly what she is hoping for.

The Students

Lorenzo is enjoying learning Italian, but he is worried about participating in class and gets very stressed when he has to turn in work for feedback because he does not want to get anything wrong. He took a chapter exam last week and just got the results back from Professoressa Feng. Although the score was excellent, he was hoping to get some additional insight into various words he could use for the same foods. Since he got a 99%, there are very few comments on his exam. Nevertheless, his success adds pressure to be consistently correct during class.

Laurene is not as happy with her score as Lorenzo. She studied very hard and used many of the same structures she had been using during group work in class. However, these were marked wrong on her exam, and she is just now finding out what she should have been saying. Also, Laurene is confused by some of the cultural information marked incorrect on her exam. For example, couldn't the ways in which people choose to apologize depend on their personalities?

Luke got an 89% on the exam and is fairly happy with the score. He breezes through it and then files it in his notebook, never to be seen again. He will study the material for the chapter 4 exam.

4.1.1 Scenario questions

1. Do Professoressa Feng's feedback practices seem similar to foreign language classrooms with which you are familiar? What are the advantages and disadvantages of her formative and summative assessment practices?
2. What are some alternative feedback methods Professoressa Feng could use, given her institutional and time constraints?
3. Are Lorenzo, Laurene, and Luke recognizable student profiles from a language classroom? What type of feedback might be more useful for each of them?
4. Some notable challenges in giving feedback for L2 learning and assessment are highlighted in this scenario. What are they? How are these similar or different from what happens in your L2TL context?

This scenario represents common challenges associated with feedback in L2TL. Under the constraints of time and course demands, educators often strive to provide individualized and meaningful feedback to students with mixed results. In this chapter, we explore ways in which a game-informed perspective on feedback can enhance and alter our understanding of feedback for L2TL. We do not advocate it as the only possible approach, but we point out ways in which game-informed pedagogy offers solutions for overcoming some of the obstacles faced by educators when providing feedback.

4.2 FEEDBACK IN L2TL

The concept of **feedback** is important in both digital games and L2TL. Just as feedback is critical to the L2TL process, effective feedback mechanisms are essential to the design of successful digital games. In game design, players are provided with consistent, individualized assistance at just the right time to be able to continue progressing in the game. Digital games encourage short-term player experimentation and failure in order to promote long-term mastery. They scaffold play by storing skills, knowledge, and resources that a player can draw on when, and only when, they are needed. These behaviors are similar to what many propose as best practice in L2TL via concepts such as *comprehensible input*, the *zone of proximal development*, *scaffolding*, and *metalinguistic learning strategies*.

In this chapter, we first briefly examine each of these L2TL theoretical constructs and relate them to the concept of *feedback as instruction*, something digital games do well. This section is followed by a game-informed discussion of the practical challenges associated with feedback in L2TL. We then explore further the complex feedback systems in digital game design with emphasis on insights for L2TL. The chapter concludes with a summary of the main points, including implications for L2TL, a new scenario, and ideas for teaching and research. As you read, we encourage you to stop to consider the "Your reflections" questions that conclude each of the sections.

4.2.1 Impact on L2 learning: Feedback as instruction

The four L2TL concepts most relevant to this chapter on feedback represent varied perspectives on interventions designed to impact a learner's L2 development, but they agree on the productive role of **feedback as instruction**. In this chapter, therefore, we do not address corrective feedback (i.e., discrete-point error correction) research, which focuses primarily on correction of grammatical errors.[1] Although digital games can be used to address development of grammatical accuracy, we focus instead on larger issues related to the place and nature of feedback in L2TL. From our perspective, a well-designed game shows us that feedback can serve as instruction by providing the resources necessary for learning. In other words, games show us that feedback can be more than just after-the-fact correction of errors.

Although they stem from different perspectives on learning, each of the concepts described here emphasizes the instructional potential of feedback in L2TL. A debate on the theoretical premises and underlying perspectives of each of these well-known principles is not the objective of this chapter and has been widely undertaken elsewhere (see, e.g., Dunn & Lantolf, 1998; Gass & Selinker, 2001; Swain, 2005). Rather, fully acknowledging possible issues of theoretical incommensurability, we highlight each concept as it speaks to a game-informed perspective, emphasizing how all share common principles with the feedback systems found in digital games.

Krashen's (1984) original hypothesis of i +1 suggests that L2 acquisition occurs as a result of learning through **comprehensible input**, in which the learner hears and acquires language that is one level above his or her own level of proficiency.[2] In other words, if input or feedback is too hard, it will be

---

[1] For a meta-analysis of corrective feedback in L2 grammar acquisition, see Russell and Spada (2006).
[2] It is important to note that Krashen's hypothesis did not include a classification of what these levels mean. This is one of the primary criticisms of Krashen's model.

over the learners' heads, but if it is fully comprehensible, it will not encourage growth by pulling the learners up. Providing input just beyond learners' abilities challenges them to keep progressing while feeling comfortable with their progress. Criticisms of the hypothesis have focused on the inexact definitions of i and 1, overemphasis on individual cognition, and no recognition of the influence of socialization and context (Dunn & Lantolf, 1998; McLaughlin, 1987; White, 1987). We concur with the myriad of criticisms of Krashen's model (e.g., de Bot, 1996; Gass & Selinker, 2001); however, we make note of the concept in this chapter because of its strong emphasis on providing feedback as a developmentally appropriate, but not overwhelming, resource.

A more precise reflection of the concept of individualized resource delivery, one that integrates the important role of social context, is Vygotsky's (1987) **zone of proximal development** (ZPD).[3] Stemming from a sociocultural perspective, Vygotsky's concept is a widely discussed aspect of development and is central to a socially informed understanding of language learning (cf. Lantolf, 2000; Lantolf & Thorne, 2006; Nassaji & Cumming, 2000). In contrast to Krashen's view of L2 acquisition as an individual cognitive phenomenon, isolated from context and based on comprehensible input, in Vygotsky's model, learning occurs via interaction with the world (i.e., other learners, experts, and surrounding contexts). Briefly, the ZPD is understood as the developmental space between what a learner can do alone and what he or she can do with help. If a learner is self-regulated, meaning that she can do an activity with no assistance or cannot do an activity even with help, then that activity is outside her ZPD. Insofar as this definition depends on the sociocultural origin of the assistance, whether another person or a cultural artifact, the ZPD can be understood as a socio-cognitive concept, rather than an individual cognitive one. Learning occurs when a learner encounters feedback at critical periods of development and in contexts where resources can be immediately applied to what is being learned. Development is sculpted by ongoing interactions in a dynamic interplay between new information and existing systems.

Related to the ZPD is the concept of **scaffolding**. From a sociocultural perspective, scaffolding is a pedagogical framework for providing feedback targeted within a learner's ZPD. When appropriately scaffolded, feedback is targeted in real time, just as it is needed. It is individualized, measured, and contextualized in interaction. Scaffolding may involve breaking down a complex activity or idea into manageable parts or providing tools such as charts, rubrics, outlines, or other organizing systems that can mediate successful completion of the activity. Learning is manageable, as the learner's working memory is not overloaded, and knowledge is distributed. Group activities can act as scaffolding, because they allow individuals to align ZPDs and share their knowledge and expertise.

A related idea to be mentioned here is the important role of learners' use of metacognitive strategies to deal with feedback. Although they do not act directly as feedback, strategies are especially crucial for the interpretation of

---

[3]See Dunn and Lantolf (1998) for a detailed comparative discussion of i +1 and Vygotsky's ZPD.

the processes occurring around the learner. As defined in Cohen (2011, p. 5), **language learning strategies** are "thoughts and actions, consciously chosen and operationalized by language learners, to assist them in carrying out a multiplicity of tasks from the very onset of learning to the most advanced levels of target-language performance." As such, they are scaffolding resources that enable the learner to deal with the multiple sources of feedback they receive in the L2 development process. For example, a learner might utilize a mnemonic device to remember and correct words to build a larger lexicon or consciously write down new structures and pragmatic strategies for future use. Learners need to develop awareness of strategies, as well as learn to use and manage them effectively.

No matter their theoretical orientation, L2TL researchers agree that feedback can, and should, serve as instruction. Feedback should be provided at the appropriate level, time, and amount for each learner. In this way, feedback serves not to judge performance but, rather, to teach. It must be meaningful, relevant, and appropriate for the action being undertaken. It also must be clear to the learner how to use the feedback for L2 learning. As we discuss later, good digital games incorporate feedback as an instruction model—games are learned as they are played. Good games are designed to provide just the right amount of information to players, pushing them along. For example, in a simple casual game, such as *Youda Sushi Chef* (Figure 4.1), players begin with two ingredients and are given more complex challenges as they progress.

FIGURE 4.1 Youda Sushi Chef *Source*: Sioux Games Production (2009).

In this way, well-designed games target the ZPDs of players, scaffold their play by storing resources and automating actions when needed, and provide a sense of agency. As noted by Gee (2003, p.1), "The secret of a videogame as a teaching machine isn't its immersive 3–D graphics, but its underlying architecture. Each level dances around the outer limits of the player's abilities, seeking at every point to be hard enough to be just doable."

4.2.2 Your reflections

1. What differences do you find in the distinction between feedback as a corrective tool and feedback as an instructional tool? Is there overlap? If so, in what ways might one complement the other?
2. Sociocultural theory provides a model for feedback as instruction that is fundamentally based in social interaction and context. What are the advantages and disadvantages of this model for L2TL?
3. What are some practical means of utilizing feedback as instruction in L2TL?

4.3 CHALLENGES FOR FEEDBACK IN L2TL

Bridging theory and practice can be a challenging endeavor in L2TL. Successful feedback as instruction as previously discussed through the ideas of i +1, the ZPD, scaffolding, and learner strategies presents a number of practical challenges in the L2 classroom, many of which can be addressed with game-informed pedagogy. These challenges include the following:

- The necessity for grades and summative assessment in some institutional contexts frames failure as error correction with a right-or-wrong message that seems to pass judgment. This approach can have a negative impact on learner motivation, resulting in a fear of failure that limits learning.
- Providing scaffolded, individualized feedback for each student can be prohibitively time consuming and unrealistic in a classroom setting.
- Giving feedback on variable language features, such as pragmatics and culture, can be problematic because there are multiple appropriate responses.
- Often the feedback given has little positive effect because it is not revisited or incorporated into future learning experiences. This lack of consequence results in low internalization, because there is no reason to pay attention to the feedback.

4.3.1 Fear of failure

The fear of failure is a common concern for students learning another language. Institutional cultures that emphasize the importance of testing and grades promote a fear of failure in students, resulting in minimized participation and risk taking, important aspects of successful L2 learning. In essence, because students perceive that each activity or assignment can potentially have a negative effect on their grade, they may perceive that even small in-class activities carry consequence. Digital games, in contrast, promote experimentation by scaffolding gameplay with instructional feedback and by allowing failure with minimal consequences.

4.3.2 Time constraints

Although many educators value feedback as instruction and scaffolding, the practical realities of a classroom do not allow for frequent individual assessments in the classroom. Instead, educators focus on systematic uses of formative assessment for periodic progress checks and high-stakes summative assessments that are more practical to administer and grade. As a result, learners do not receive the timely, individualized feedback that is important for their L2 development. Instead, feedback comes in periodic segments, often one to two weeks after the action itself. Good digital games, in contrast, are able to individualize feedback just when it is needed, because of their digital nature. This **just-in-time** quality, by which we mean timely, measured feedback delivered immediately at the moment of trial, is crucial to the effectiveness of feedback. Moreover, a single, well-designed digital game can be played whenever and as many times as needed. It can store unique data on each player, resulting in a different, customized play experience for each one.

4.3.3 Language variation

Another difficult challenge in assessing and giving feedback as instruction is the treatment of language variation. As a result of the inherent nature of many of the perceptions we have about the context of interaction, it is especially difficult to determine whether a learner is making an error based on lack of knowledge or understanding or whether the deviation from the norm is intentional (e.g., Bardovi-Harlig, 2001). Thus, attention to the social context, personality, and personal choice of the learner is critical. Subjectivity, as defined by Ishihara and Tarone (2009), reflects learners' choices about the language behaviors they adopt as related to their own self-identity, values, beliefs, morals, feelings, and personal principles. Subjectivity has been shown to have a profound impact on, for example, pragmatic choices (Cohen, 1997; LoCastro, 2003). Nevertheless, focusing on subjectivity and language variation in the L2 classroom while also allowing multiple correct options can be impractical and overwhelming. In contrast, digital games can account for multiple correct answers and give various forms of feedback that expand beyond a binary right/wrong approach, well beyond the capacity of a single teacher, again because of their digital nature.

4.3.4 Low consequence and internalization

In many cases, feedback given on exams, compositions, and other high-stakes assignments occurs after the fact and aside from its impact on a learner's grade, has limited impact on the learner's development. When feedback is untimely and not recycled into further learning, internalization is minimal. In good digital games, by contrast, real-time immediate feedback is a foundational mechanism that promotes successful gameplay and internalization, because the player perceives a sense of agency with every choice, and choices are discernable and integrated (see Section 4.4.2). At the same time, as Prensky (2001, p. 123) notes: "Game players are in some sense 'protected' from the dangers of the real world. While this is certainly true physically, it does not necessarily apply to players' emotions while playing the game, which are very real indeed." In other words, no tangible risks are associated with the virtual experience, making risk taking and experimentation positive experiences. This allows for failure to occur as a primary means of instruction. At the same time, authentic emotions and real-world reactions guide gameplay and help the learner internalize feedback. Furthermore, in some digital games, interactions with other players can add an additional level of authenticity to the experience.

4.3.5 Your reflections

1. Do you agree that these practical challenges associated with feedback as instruction in L2TL exist? Why or why not? Can you think of other challenges we have not mentioned?
2. Is there a fear of failure in your educational context? If so, what could you do to encourage more experimentation?
3. Aside from digital games, what other solutions are available for overcoming these challenges in providing feedback?

4.4 FEEDBACK IN DIGITAL GAMES

The feedback systems in digital games are fundamental aspects of game design and gameplay. They not only guide the players in successfully navigating the digital space, but also play a significant role in the player's decision to continue playing or abandon the game, contributing to the *flow* experience of the player (Czikszentmihalyi, 2008; see Chapter 6). As we discussed in Chapter 2, if a game is too easy, it is boring and likely not interesting to the player; yet, if it is too hard, often the result of inadequate feedback, the game quickly becomes frustrating. The feedback system in a digital game not only teaches players how to play, making them expert players, but also keeps players playing, even in instances of intensely difficult or challenging gameplay. In this section, we explore four underlying concepts of integrated feedback systems in digital games that are especially relevant to our current discussion—*fail states, discernability, positive and negative feedback*, and *feedback through social interaction*. As we explore these concepts, we encourage you to reflect on how each might connect to our previous discussion of challenges in feedback and L2TL.

4.4.1 How do digital games utilize fail states as opportunities for feedback?

A fundamental of any game system is the inherent opportunity for failure with unlimited attempts for replay and improvement—this is the concept of **fail states**. A player may attempt a task as many times as he or she wishes and often receives feedback from multiple sources to improve when the outcome is unsatisfactory. Although failure often comes with consequences, there is almost always a chance to retry after an unsuccessful endeavor. These consequences are congruent with the level of error made by the player. When selecting tasks, a player must evaluate the risk associated with a certain task and then choose which tasks to complete when (see Chapter 2 for a discussion of task choice). Consistent, real-time, and meaningful feedback is critical to allow players to make these choices. When a player fails, feedback is always salient to help the player retry and progress. For example, in the majority of adventure games, the player must search for clues and find specific items to move forward. This may mean entering dangerous places and exploring new realms. Exploration and experimentation may result in many missed attempts prior to finding the correct place. After each missed attempt, the game gives feedback as to what went wrong, as well as clues for moving forward, each time encouraging the player to continue experimenting. The inherent nature of fail states in digital games pushes the player to keep playing and improving each step along the way. Errors are accepted and, at the same time, corrected via numerous mechanisms through a series of low-stakes tasks. These smaller tasks support the player by building his or her repertoire and, eventually, the combination of the skills built during the various failed attempts enables the player to complete a larger, high-stakes task. For example, in *Farm Frenzy 3*, a casual farming action-simulation game (Figure 4.2), players complete a series of small farming tasks (represented

FIGURE 4.2 Farm Frenzy 3 This image is from the Russian version of the game.
Source: Alawar Entertainment, Inc. (2011).

by each of the circles) that culminate in the final task (the completion of all circles that moves them on to the next large farm). These larger tasks, often called boss levels, are often more difficult to accomplish and, if completed successfully, result in greater rewards (e.g., items, bonus points). Likewise, the consequences of failure are often much higher.

This reliance on fail states to provide feedback closely parallels the socio-cultural understanding of L2 development, whereby "accents, (un)grammaticality, and pragmatic and lexical failures are not just flaws or signs of imperfect learning but ways in which learners attempt to establish (new) identities and gain self-regulation through linguistic means" (Dunn & Lantolf, 1998, p. 428). On the other hand, this perspective stands in stark contrast to the belief that the purpose of feedback in the L2 classroom is to ensure that errors do not recur, which reflects a stimulus-response theory of learning and is based on fear of failure. From this view, more systematic feedback is reserved for high-stakes assessments such as unit tests and oral exams, and inaccuracy is immediately labeled a learning failure on the part of the student.

In a well-designed game, it is difficult to miss the feedback that is given from multiple sources; however, the complexity and interactivity of the feedback create loops and are, therefore, difficult to isolate. In the sections that follow, we attempt to unpack the ways in which feedback is structured and designed in digital games with the ultimate goal of highlighting features that are especially relevant for L2TL.

4.4.2 How do digital games give individualized, just-in-time feedback?

One essential element of any successful digital game is **discernability**, the ability of the player to determine "the immediate outcome of any action" (Salen & Zimmerman, 2004, p. 35). In other words, a player knows immediately if his or her action has been successful and, in many cases, simultaneously receives systematic feedback from a variety of sources. As a result, each individual player gets the feedback necessary to continue moving forward, no matter his or her skill level, either by repeating the same task to improve or by moving on to a more challenging quest. We see this system of feedback clearly in *Youda Sushi Chef*, a casual action-management game in which the player combines ingredients to make various types of sushi that are ordered in the restaurant (Figure 4.1). The bar at the top of the screen gives players feedback via a star rating, a meter of materials and energy, and coins that they earn. Each customer also has a happiness meter above his or her image to indicate how well the player is doing making the sushi in real time.

In some single-player games, this real-time feedback adapts to a specific skill level of the player, using intelligent tutor technology (Prensky, 2006) called **dynamic difficulty assessment** (DDA). In DDA, the game itself adds or eliminates extra resources based on the success or failure of a previous quest, creating a personalized gameplay experience.

In addition to being individualized and discernable for each player, feedback is delivered exactly at the moment it is needed, not too soon and not too late, resulting in a just-in-time feedback mechanism that is powerful for target-ing each player's individual actions. In doing so, the feedback given and the expectations of success are suited to the level of the player. Feedback delivered in this way is meaningful to the player because it is immediately relevant to the task at hand, and the skills learned are critical for moving forward and ulti-mately reaching the endgame point. This individualized, just-in-time model is a practical manifestation of the ideal theoretical models of the ZPD and scaffold-ing, whereby each learner is given just the right amount and type of assistance at the right time to maximize his or her learning experience.

4.4.3 How is feedback in digital games designed?

Feedback type and design are different in every game, with some games offering more levels of complexity than others. Salen and Zimmerman (2004) highlight the complexities associated with feedback systems in digital games. They describe a series of cybernetic systems that are connected to one another in the majority of digital games. On a basic level, these systems are either **positive feedback systems**, which give a certain advantage that makes the system unstable, or **negative feedback systems**, which re-stabilize the sys-tem by taking away certain advantages. They often work together to maintain balance in the game, pushing the player forward and holding him or her back when needed. For example, the popular MMOG *World of Warcraft (WoW)* takes advantage of a number of positive and negative feedback systems to guide the player. If a player ventures too far outside of his designated play-ing area, he draws *aggro* (i.e., aggression) from the enemies in the area. The enemies immediately note a low-level player in the area and focus their atten-tion, usually killing the player immediately. In doing so, the player is given real-time negative feedback that he is in the wrong area. The immediate attack suggests it would be better to play in another place where the levels of the player and the enemies are comparable. This negative feedback loop restores balance to the system by making it difficult for players to wander too far from the play area where they can feasibly win battles against enemies. At the same time, positive feedback systems provide assets that offer a profound advantage to the player. For example, when in the appropriate area, a *WoW* player may encounter enemies at, just below, or just above his or her level. This feature of the game makes it possible to take risks and gain skills by defeating enemies that are within the player's ZPD. This being said, we should note that game design does not necessarily guarantee a certain gameplay experience; players often flout the systems and attempt various tasks that are far above or below their abilities, despite the in-game feedback. Even so, the feedback mechanisms exist and are intended as salient guidance for all players.

As each of these systems functions, the player is made explicitly aware of what is happening as a result of his or her actions. Feedback, utilizing a posi-tive or negative feedback loop, is delivered to a player via a variety of salient **feedback mechanisms**. Some of the most common feedback mechanisms are described in Table 4.1.

Table 4.1 Feedback Mechanisms in Digital Games

Feedback Mechanism	Description	Example
Leveling	Leveling demonstrates how far the player is progressing toward a next step. It typically does not decrease.	In *World of Warcraft*, a player works through a total of 80 levels to reach the endgame point. This endgame level is sometimes raised with expansions to the game as more and more players look for a continued challenging experience.
Points	Points are usually given on a numeric scale, increasing as the player does better and often decreasing when the player makes a mistake.	In *Angry Birds*, a player strives for a high score on a variety of levels. Although points are accumulated, they restart at the beginning of each level.
Asset building	Assets are in-game resources that a player receives, often as part of collections, that can be stored and used at a later time. They can grant, for example, special skills, access to different locations, and the ability to use other items.	In *Mario Kart*, players collect various items to help them in the race by hitting question mark squares. The various items can be used at strategic times to enable the racer to beat other faster cars.
Skill building	As a player practices and becomes better at a skill, feedback is given in the form of a progress bar, points, or level to indicate expertise in the skill. In some instances, the skill feedback is distinct from leveling; in other cases, it is one and the same.	In *Runescape*, a player chooses skills to master such as cooking, construction, magic, or prayer.
Tips and hints	Games build in clues that guide a player through the necessary steps to complete a task. They often appear after the player has made a mistake.	In *Super Mario Brothers*, the Toad character often steps in to help players who are lost, teach new skills, and work with a player toward mastery.
Real-time progress bars	Short-term progress bars often track a player's progress for a specific period of time or in specific place while completing a specific activity. Bars often reset after the player has succeeded or failed at the activity.	During a duel in *Everquest*, the player has a lifeline that decreases as he or she gets attacked. It resets and disappears upon completion of the duel.
Sound effects	Games use auditory cues to indicate correct or incorrect actions.	In *Lifequest*, an alarm clock buzz is used to indicate that the player is running out of time and may lose additional time to play the next day.
Active and inactive game elements	Objects and characters are active only when needed. An element's interactivity helps indicate when the player is on the correct or incorrect path.	In *Plants vs. Zombies*, only plants that are relevant to the place being planted can be used. Choices are guided through the available and unavailable plants.

FIGURE 4.3 Mentira *Source*: Holden and Sykes (2011).

Even the simplest of digital games use a minimum of three of these mechanisms; the majority make use of all of them. Multiple sources of feedback allow players to track all of their skills, abilities, assets, and actions at the same time, while still focusing on the elements they need at each moment. In *Mentira*, a mobile adventure game-based L2 learning environment, players do this through an inventory mechanism in which they collect clues and assets and then decide what they need to solve the murder mystery. Figure 4.3 depicts a sample inventory screen from the middle of the game. In this case, the player has collected historical artifacts, a family card, and various clues that will be needed for solving the murder.

We imagine the use of multiple feedback mechanisms in L2TL to enable learners to track their language development from a variety of perspectives consistently, in real time as they are learning, not only when they have a mistake corrected or when they get their tests back.

4.4.4 How is feedback given in player interactions?

Especially prevalent in digital games with large followings, the final type of feedback is given by expert members of player communities to novice members via interaction through, around, and about the game (see Chapters 3 and 5 for discussions of these types of interactions and contexts). These are most common in MMOGs (through and around the game) and complex single-player commercial games (about the game, often in online fora)—they are not usually associated with casual games. As players involved with a game, they interact with other players about the game and receive useful feedback about appropriate actions, behaviors, and strategies from a community of expert players. For example, in *WoW*, new players are often identified in-game by their mistakes, and learn the rules of interaction from experienced players. Through this apprenticeship process, they also learn how to be expert members of the community (Lave & Wenger, 1991). Player interaction thus adds an additional level of authentic feedback that can be used (or not used) by players to enhance their digital gameplay experience. The importance of incorporating access to, analysis of, and participation in these interactions has been discussed at length by L2TL researchers, and it should be considered an important source of feedback (Thorne, Black, & Sykes, 2009; Thorne and Reinhardt, 2008; Thorne, Reinhardt, and Golombek, 2008).

4.4.5 Your reflections

1. What is your experience with feedback in L2TL? In your opinion, what are L2 instructors' perspectives on errors? How might a game-informed perspective on fail states change the dynamics of L2TL learning experiences?
2. In the L2 classroom, what could be considered the equivalent of positive and negative feedback systems? Consider, for example, extra credit, or a pop quiz. In what ways does L2TL benefit from each type of feedback loop?
3. Look at the feedback types in Table 4.1. Which may have parallels in traditional L2 feedback mechanisms? Which do not? How could each type be adapted to L2TL contexts?
4. In a digital game–mediated curriculum, how could you take advantage of game communities as a source of feedback for L2TL?

4.5 SUMMARY AND IMPLICATIONS

The following list summarizes the main points of this chapter on feedback, with implications for transformed L2TL:

1. A good feedback-as-instruction model focuses on providing individualized resources to learners at the right amount, level, and time. The feedback must be meaningful, relevant, and appropriate for the action being undertaken.
2. Although the theoretical importance of instructional feedback systems has been established in the L2TL literature, their practical application presents a number of challenges, including overcoming learner fear of failure, practical time constraints, difficulties with language variation, and the low impact of after-the-fact feedback.
3. A balance between boredom and frustration is maintained, in part, by the use of complex feedback loops. A strong balance that challenges the player at just the right level contributes to a sense of flow.
4. Fail states serve as the primary underlying mechanism driving the form of feedback given to the player. Digital games use these individualized, just-in-time feedback systems to develop player expertise.

5. Positive and negative feedback loops utilizing multiple feedback mechanisms form the underlying learning system of a digital game. Similar systems have the potential to be especially powerful for L2TL.

6. Feedback offered in player interaction and participation in attendant discourses and player communities can be a powerful resource for L2TL.

7. Digital games incorporate a practical, systematic implementation of concepts that have parallels in some models of SLA and L2 pedagogy. Utilizing digital game mechanisms, practitioners have the tools to enhance feedback in L2TL, and realize its capacity for effective instruction, rather than just for assessment.

4.6 A GAME-INFORMED SCENARIO: *THE GOLDEN TREASURE*

After grading the chapter 3 exams, Professoressa Feng can feel the challenges her students are facing. She knows that something needs to change in the way she gives feedback, and she remembers that a student once mentioned how great digital games were at helping a player get better. She decides to check a few out and work with her students, Lorenzo, Laurene, and Luke, to design a feedback system that would enhance her language course for the next semester. Over the summer, she and her students play a number of complex digital games and start to notice how feedback is used to help players become better. They then design a model to help transfer some of these behaviors to the Italian classroom. Professoressa Feng's feedback model for the new semester includes the following:

- She develops two point systems: *punti d'oro* (gold points) and *punti d'argento* (silver points), whereby 1 gold point is worth 10 silver points. Students earn gold points from tests and class assignments, and they earn silver points from class participation, assisting other students, risk taking (e.g., speaking first to answer an open question), using feedback given on assignments, participating in out-of-class sessions, and doing extra-credit assignments. Gold points are permanent, but students can lose silver points by not attending to feedback, or by losing them in duels (see later discussion). She creates a chart on the course website that shows how much every class activity is worth. Students can also check the website to see their progress.

- Based on the curriculum objectives, she develops another system of *tesori* (treasures) as pictures on cards, and she awards them for a 100% score on small quizzes and assignments. These are listed on the website. For example, a *smeraldo* (emerald) is awarded for a quiz on *avere* (have) conjugations, and a *pozione* (potion) is awarded for a composition describing one's family. Students may repeat a quiz or assignment as many times as they like until they earn the *tesori*, and they may exchange each one for the number of silver points that she determines for each individual.

- She creates a duel system, whereby students, as individuals or teams, may challenge one another to duel for silver points and treasures once a week. Duels typically focus on more complex language structures or cultural elements of language.
- She creates a level system, mirroring the Italian nobility title system: *cavaliere, barone, visconte, conte, marchese, duca,* and *principe* (including feminine versions), in which each corresponds to a different number of points. Students level up as they accumulate points. Students can check their levels on the website, and they receive a certificate whenever they gain a new title. She uses the students' final point tally to determine a component of their final grade.

After working with Professoressa Feng over the summer, Lorenzo, Laurene, and Luke are looking forward to the upcoming year and decide to enroll in Italian 2 to see how the system works. Lorenzo finds himself advancing more quickly then he had been previously and experimenting with language in ways he was scared to do at earlier levels. His test scores remain high, but he is more willing to speak up in class. He won a duel with Luke for a *calice* (chalice) by naming five Italian regions in 15 seconds. Laurene now knows where she stands, and she has posted her *marchessa* certificate on her Facebook profile. She still struggles with language, but she attends the out-of-class sessions once a week to gain more points. Luke now saves all of the feedback given on tests and assignments because he is intent on becoming a *principe*. He is earning a lot of silver points by helping other students in the out-of-class sessions. For her part, Professoressa Feng is trying to use the system to provide feedback to students when they need it, and to reward them when they use it. She spends a lot of time developing and fine-tuning the new system, but she has realized that time spent now will save her time later. The more numerous smaller activities are a lot of work, and it is sometimes a challenge to note who has earned which points when. Still, she sees the students' motivation increasing and has a much better idea of where they stand individually, and where they need assistance.

4.6.1 Scenario questions

1. What is your reaction to the game-informed scenario? Does it seem realistic for L2TL?
2. Does this new model cover all of the elements of a meaningful feedback system—individualized, just-in-time, scaffolded, and relevant? If so, in what ways? If not, in what ways could it be improved?
3. Some may argue the system proposed by Professoressa Feng is just about entertainment and fun, and not about learning. Do you agree or disagree? Why?
4. How might students be taught to learn in this game-informed feedback system? What would be the challenges of teaching students how to use it?

4.7 GAME-MEDIATED APPLICATIONS

In this section, we offer three applications of the concepts surrounding feedback from this chapter. Each is derived as a specific example of the general implementation model from the book: game-enhanced, game-based, and game-informed L2TL. We first present a game-enhanced activity focusing on feedback in vernacular games. We then present a template for designing feedback in a game-based environment and then offer final reflection questions and ideas for game-informed pedagogy.

4.7.1 A game-enhanced activity focusing on feedback

The objective of this set of activities is to focus learners on the various feedback mechanisms in vernacular games with the goal of improving their language learning skills. The first activity focuses learners on in-game feedback and the second on the attendant discourses of associated communities. Through analysis of the various ways feedback is given (in-game and via surrounding communities), students become more aware of the multitude of feedback mechanisms available to them in the L2 learning process as well as the language behaviors of the attendant discourses of communities associated with vernacular games.

Procedures
1. Choose two games for learners to play in the target language. See Appendix II: Guide to Game Types and Genres to help in your selection of a genre and type for use in this activity. We suggest selecting a game that has a strong player community for this activity. Traditionally, these are MMOGs, some social networking games, and simulation games such as *The SIMS*. This community will be critical in completing the second activity in this series.
2. Introduce the activity in class with special emphasis on feedback and the places learners can gain feedback on their language learning process. For example, you might focus on the lexical items needed to complete the task and the feedback that is given by the game when the wrong word is used or understood. Alternatively, you might help learners pay attention to the points in the game where feedback is given and highlight the language important to each of these points. This can include a brainstorming session of feedback sources and explicit instruction of metalinguistic strategies. Ask learners to make a list of what they will gain from this activity.
3. Have learners play the selected game for approximately 30 minutes without any interference from the instructor. Depending on the institutional and cultural constraints, this can be done in class or as homework.
4. After students play the game individually, present Activity 4A to guide them in noticing the type of feedback available in the game. You may use Table 4.1 as a resource to help them distinguish feedback types.

5. In groups, have learners return to the game they originally played and complete Activity 4A. This additional play session allows learners to focus on the analysis component after already being familiar with the game. After all of the groups have finished, discuss their findings and ways the game might benefit their own language learning experiences. Questions may include the following:

    a. Do students think the game could be helpful for own language learning? Why or why not?

    b. Are certain components of the game a good and/or not-so-good fit between the language features accessed in the game and the students' own strengths and weaknesses?

    c. Where is the feedback most and least relevant?

    These can then be highlighted as possible resources for additional L2 learning and paralleled with other feedback mechanisms outside of the game itself.

6. After addressing various elements of feedback in the game, through Activity 4A, have learners examine how feedback is given and taken by members of the surrounding community (see Chapter 3 for additional information on attendant discourses). Activity 4B serves as a guide for linguistic observation and processing of attendant discourses.

7. After learners have completed Activity 4B, discuss the findings as a class with special attention to the way feedback is given to members of the community. Sample questions include the following:

    a. Are there specific linguistic strategies that are more or less effective? Why might this be?

    b. Are there certain communicative functions (e.g., requests, apologies, suggestions) that are especially relevant to this discourse community? What are some strategies members of the community use to carry out these functions?

    c. How do members of the community give feedback on each other's language and ideas?

Notes

- Critical to the success of these activities is the selection of appropriate games. An active community is needed to complete Activity 4B. These communities are not usually associated with casual games. Therefore, complex games such as MMOGs and simulations will be more effective.
- Depending on the level of the learner, these activities can be completed in the target language, the students' native language, or a combination of the two.
- Sample analyses of different games might be helpful if learners are having difficulty.
- Activity 4B can serve as a springboard for further analysis of interactional features such as communicative acts, politeness, and persuasive discourse.

ACTIVITY 4A

In-game feedback

How do you know how well you are doing in the game?

After playing [the game], complete the following chart with your group:

List in this column all of the feedback mechanisms you find in the game. For each mechanism, answer the questions.	What is the purpose of this feedback mechanism? Does it serve its purpose well?	What does the feedback help you learn? What does it not help you learn? Is this effective for your L2 development?	How does this feedback mechanism compare to other feedback mechanisms in your L2 learning experience?

ACTIVITY 4B

Feedback in player interactions: An analysis task

Examine at least three online discussions or interactions related to the game you have been playing. Based on your observations, answer the following questions:

1. What strategies do players use to give feedback?
2. What strategies do players use to respond to feedback?
3. What language do you notice that might be helpful?
4. List any expressions, words, or structures related to feedback that you do not understand.
5. How could you use what you have learned here to give and get feedback on the language you are learning?
6. Do you have any other observations?

4.7.2 Designing a game-based L2TL environment: Focus on feedback

As in previous chapters, this section focuses on the design of one specific element of the game, in this case, feedback. It should be used in conjunction with the content from the other sections you have worked on (e.g., goals, interaction). In this section, we offer a framework that designers, instructors, and learners can use to think about feedback in the design of game-based L2TL environments (i.e., SIEs). Depending on the level of the learners, the whole activity can be completed in the target language, or specific elements can be designated as "target language only."

Procedures

1. Prepare, modify, and translate the activity sheet as necessary.

2. In class, explain to the students that they will be helping design a digital game for language learning and will be focusing on feedback. This activity can be done in conjunction with the other design activities in other chapters or on its own.

3. Explain the objectives of the activity—to develop critical awareness about games, rethink feedback for language learning to be more effective, and design target language expressions to give feedback.

4. Have students complete the activities from Section 4.6.1 so they better understand the way feedback works in digital games.

5. Have learners work in groups to complete the activity.

CHAPTER 4   Game design activity: Design a digital game to learn [insert language]—Focus on feedback

You have been given a grant to build a digital game that will help students learn [insert language]. One step in the design process is to come up with types of feedback that will instruct and motivate players. As a group, design the feedback mechanisms of your game by answering the following questions. Be sure to include as many details as possible.

1.   Basic Information
     a. What will you learn?
     b. What type of game is it (e.g., simulation, adventure)?
     c. What is the object of the game (what a player does to win)?
     d. What is the context of the game (setting, characters, etc.)?
2.   Feedback
     a. What sorts of feedback mechanisms are used to guide the player through your game?
     b. Choose three mechanisms and describe each one by answering the following questions:
          i.   What is the mechanism?
          ii. How is it presented to players (e.g., progress bar, money)?
          iii. What does the player do to receive feedback?
          iv. What is the intention of the feedback? What does it tell the player?
          v.   How does the feedback mechanism help the players learn?
          vi. How does the feedback mechanism motivate players to keep playing?
3.   Create a screenshot that demonstrates the three feedback mechanisms you have described.
4.   Write accompanying dialogue for each feedback mechanism. (e.g., Great job! Try again! Have you thought about . . . ? Maybe you'll have better luck if . . .).

4.7.3 Your game-informed reflections

A game-informed approach suggests a reconceptualization of feedback in L2TL. It is not embodied in one specific technique or method. Reflect on the chapter and consider the following topics:

1. Think about a particular class or course and the ways that feedback was delivered. Were you satisfied with the feedback you gave or received? Why or why not? How might a game-informed approach have changed this experience?

2. Consider a traditional first-year language course with four chapter exams, a midterm, and a final exam. How might a game-informed approach change this model? What would be the advantages and disadvantages?

3. Fail states are a critical component of successful games and of learning in game-based environments. Design one activity for the classroom that takes advantage of the positive power of experimentation and making mistakes.

4. How could you incorporate game-informed feedback mechanisms— individualized, scaffolded, complex—into your classroom without the use of digital games? How might the use of digital games enhance this pedagogy?

5. In what ways might game-based feedback allow you to address language variation in the classroom? What are some practical techniques you could use to further address language variation?

6. Action research is critical to furthering our understanding of feedback in digital game-mediated L2TL. What types of research projects would be most helpful? How would you investigate, for example, the effectiveness of in-game feedback? Game-informed in-class feedback? The design of feedback mechanisms for specific language features? The complexity and leveling of feedback most effective for language learning?

. . . . . . ▬▬▬▬▬▬▬▬▬▬▬▬▬▬▬▬▬▬▬

Context
The role of narrative

5.1 A SCENARIO: *THE PROMISE OF NARRATIVES*

Ikegami-sensei

In a fifth-semester university Japanese classroom, Ikegami-sensei is thinking about how she will maintain her students' interest when she introduces a reading that is longer than usual next week. It is part of the curriculum, but, over the years, she has found that many students lose interest when she introduces longer pieces. She explains to the students that it is important to be familiar with some foundational pieces of literature, and she starts with simplified versions of twentieth-century pieces, hoping to keep students interested. The best students seem to follow, but most of the others trail off. She has thought of doing some pieces with *manga* (i.e., Japanese comics), but she tends to agree with some of her colleagues that they should introduce pop culture pieces in addition to, but not in place of, foundational literature. She has taught lower levels using Japanese fairy tales, and she found that most students enjoyed them, although a few found them childish. In any case, she is thinking of allowing the students to use translations with the tougher pieces, in the hope that this will help the students understand them better.

The Students

Cindy has taken four semesters of Japanese and visited Japan for a summer study abroad program. She is still in contact with many of her Japanese friends, and she enjoys speaking the language, although she finds reading and writing more challenging. After her experience in Japan, she is a bit more critical of lessons during which students have to read pieces from traditional works of literature. Once she was in Japan, she found that she enjoyed reading (or trying to read) popular magazines and manga, and that both gave her something to talk about with her friends.

Roberta visited Japan in high school, and she is thinking about doing a double major in Japanese and art. She is very interested in *anime* (Japanese animation) and Japanese fan culture, and she was happy when an instructor in a previous class had activities involving popular *anime* cartoons. She has written some fan fiction about her favorite *anime* characters, but only in English with a few Japanese words thrown in here or there.

Peter was convinced to take Japanese past the basic language requirement because of his love of Japanese video games. He has tried to play some on his own in Japanese. He has found that when he masters a particular game in English, he can then play the game in Japanese with the help of a dictionary. He has also found a few websites with discussion boards frequented by American gamers who like Japanese games, and he enjoys following the discussions and reading gaming tips.

5.1.1 Scenario questions

1. What are the main curricular demands of intermediate and advanced language courses, and how are they different from those of basic language courses? How do instructors usually approach these challenges, and how do students respond?
2. What approaches and techniques for teaching literature in the L2 classroom are you familiar with? In your experience as an instructor or learner, which are effective, and why? What issues are there with less commonly taught L2s, and L2s with non-Roman writing systems?
3. How are the students in this scenario similar to or different from those you have known as a learner or instructor? What are their reasons for studying the language, and what sorts of activities do you think they would find meaningful and interesting?

This scenario presents an L2TL situation familiar to many, in particular, an instructor faced with the literature-oriented demands of a high-intermediate curriculum. These more advanced courses often have trouble attracting and maintaining sufficient student enrollment because of the dramatic shift between the kinds of activities common in lower-level courses and those related to literature-oriented, higher-level courses. Intermediate- and advanced-level activities tend to be more literature focused, sometimes implemented using more traditional approaches such as grammar–translation. Unfortunately, these approaches often decontextualize the target language in ways that make it difficult for students who cannot relate to the context of the narratives or lessons presented.

Although digital games will never replace all literary content, they can complement it with contexts and narratives that are familiar to learners and that can be connected to traditional literature and literature-oriented approaches. Digital games and traditional literary works have the potential to complement one another. Moreover, games may inform our understanding of the role of context in learning and may offer transformative insights into how we teach narrative in the L2 classroom.

5.2 CONTEXT AND NARRATIVE

In this chapter, we explore another common area between L2TL and digital games—the central role of context in both learning a language and playing a digital game. A digital game is composed of a designed context, an environment that is in some ways self-contained; in the same way, a lesson or unit of L2 instruction is also self-contained. However, as discussed in Chapter 3, game developers also consider the importance of social and cultural interactivity in game design, just as many linguists consider language use to involve not just ideational but also interpersonal and textual meaning (e.g., Halliday, 1978). In games, it is not just the designed context, what we might call the **context-in-the-game**, but also the **context of play** (i.e., where, with whom, and for what reasons one plays) that creates meaning for the player. We believe this understanding of context has useful implications for L2TL.

Some linguists argue that a word or utterance has meaning out of its context of use, no matter who says it or the circumstances around it. According to this structural perspective, the statement "the apple is blue," for example, is understandable independently of context, because most native speakers of English know what "apples" are, and what the meaning of "blue" is. However, if we try to learn a foreign language this way, relying only on direct translation, we will probably fail in the long run. When figuring out meaning, we use contextual clues, so that if one knows the meaning of "apple" but not "blue," one might think it means "red," because we know that most apples are red. In other words, meaning is always understood in relationship to other concepts, within contexts of understanding. Audiolingualism, a structural approach to L2TL popularized in the 1960s, had learners repeat structures over and over with the goal that repetition would result in habit formation (Larsen-Freeman & Anderson, 2011). It had poor results in terms of attaining advanced proficiency, however, perhaps because the repetitions were rarely connected to a context that was meaningful to the learner. It is impossible to move beyond surface-level meaning without recognizing context.

Before it is played, a digital game is a designed context composed of rules and narratives. Game rules are abstract until narrative contextualizes them, usually with a combination of language and graphical imagery that paints a picture or tells a story. For example, a management game might challenge you to run a successful bakery (e.g., *Bakery Story, Maggie's Bakery*), where you might have to make an increasingly varied number of pies, cakes, and cookies to level up and win. By directing you to make a pie with red apples, red cherries, and green apples, the game provides a context for you to use those concepts meaningfully. In this way, the bakery narrative is central to the game design, as well as the means through which you learn to play it.

Game developers work with the understanding that games have both a designed context-in-the-game and an emergent context of play. In the self-contained designed context, players learn rules by experiencing them through meaningful narratives. At the same time, the game does not exist outside of a context of play, and the true meaning of the game is not realized until it is played by somebody, somewhere, and for some reason. This fundamental dual conceptualization of context is the subject of this chapter. We believe it can inform, and potentially transform, L2TL.

To introduce this idea, we first discuss how context is understood in linguistics and L2TL. We then present two contrasting understandings of language—structural and functional perspectives. This includes a discussion of the functional understanding of context as being both situational and cultural. We then present the concept of narrative and how it is considered an important, if not the most important, way we learn. This is followed by a discussion of how the field of games studies has looked at narrative, and why narrative is a key aspect of game design. Finally, we offer implications for L2TL, followed by a summary of the main points of the chapter, a new scenario, and ideas for teaching and research. As you read, we encourage you to stop and ponder the questions for discussion and reflection that are at the end of the sections ("Your reflections").

5.2.1 Context in linguistics and L2TL

The idea of **context** is understood differently in various approaches to linguistics. According to most **structural** linguists, a language at its core is a grammar. Structural analyses often include the use of abstract formulae and examples that represent the grammar rules underlying a particular language. For example, English word order is subject–verb–object (SVO), adjectives come before the nouns they modify (Adj+N), and prepositions come before their objects, which are nouns (Prep+N). In Japanese, by contrast, word order is subject–object–verb (SOV), adjectives are pre-nominal as in English, and prepositions are actually post-positions, because they come after their objects, although they are usually categorized as particles (N+part). Lexical items can be fit into these formulae like puzzles. These items have semantic qualities, or meanings, that combine to produce discourse. From this modular view, once these rules and vocabulary are memorized, texts can theoretically be translated, regardless of whether the translator understands the meaning of what he or she is saying. Context is thought of as another level on top of the foundation of syntax and semantics, related to pragmatics, yet not necessarily part of the core system.

From a social perspective, context is at the core and is key to both using and learning language. As such, it cannot be ignored. From our first language experience as infants, when we make a connection between an object or action and the utterance our caretaker uses to refer to it, contextualized use is the natural way we learn meaning. Good teachers know that L2 learning should be based on use and that all L2 use should be contextualized. In practice, however, producing contextualized experiences in a language classroom is difficult because the classroom is a rather artificial environment for talking about objects other than desks, clocks, and books. It is no coincidence that school supplies and numbers are the first vocabulary our students learn successfully in the target language. Although most students can make abstract connections to objects outside the classroom, usually with the help of realia, pictures, and video, some students have difficulty making the leap to meaningful language use. Study abroad experiences are one way to enhance the role of context in L2TL, but it may not be an economic or practical reality for all language learners. In general, formal L2TL context is the classroom, no matter how hard the instructor and learners try to imagine otherwise.

In contrast to structuralists, **functional** linguists theorize that language has meaning only in the situation in which it occurs, the **context of situation** (Malinowski, 1923), or the "environment of the text" (Halliday and Hasan, 1989). Halliday's (1978) three functions, discussed in Chapter 3, correspond to three aspects of context of situation—ideational meaning is the field of the text or usage event, interpersonal is the tenor, and textual is the mode. In the classroom, even when teachers are able to make the ideational field of a text understood, that is, its basic transactional meaning, the interpersonal tenor is still usually defined by the teacher-student relationship, even if learners are told to imagine otherwise. The mode of a particular text, that is, its relationship to broader discourses and contexts, is also difficult to establish when teachers present utterances out of context—for example, to illustrate a grammatical point.

The context of situation has great influence on the meaning of a particular text or language-use event. Hymes (1972) uses the acronym SPEAKING to explain the variety of contextual features that can impact meaning—*s*etting, *p*articipants, the *e*nds or purposes, *a*ct sequences or schemata, the *k*ey or tone, *i*nstrumentalities, *n*orms of interaction, and *g*enre:

- *Setting* refers to the place and time that the text or event occurs.
- *Participants* refers to the individuals present and referred to.
- *Ends* or *purposes* refers to the pragmatic intention of the text, that is, what the speaker intends it to accomplish and how the listener interprets that intention.
- *Act sequences* refers to the generic structure of the event, that is, in what stage of the discourse it occurs.
- *Key* or *tone* refers to the paralinguistic qualities of the text, for example, if it is whispered or read ironically.
- *Instrumentalities* refers to the register of the text, for example, the channel or the speech variety used.
- *Norms* refer to the permissible interaction structures of the event. For example, in a dialogue, both listener and speaker are meant to contribute, whereas in a speech, only the speaker does so.
- *Genre* refers to the kind of text, or the text type, as particular discourse communities recognize it.

On a broader level, every situation also occurs on a cultural level—the **context of culture**. It is easy to imagine how each feature of Hymes's definition of context may differ across cultures, and how one participant's expectations of each feature may differ from those of another. Pragmatic and intercultural misunderstandings often occur because even if the situational meaning of a text is understood, its cultural context may not be. In other words, even if we can recreate a genuine context of language use in the L2TL environment, the cultural context may still be inauthentic or not authenticated by learners (see Chapter 2, Chapter 6).

Learning an L2 without context is difficult because natural language use always occurs in a context of situation and, on a broader level, of culture. At the same time, learning is facilitated when it is situated in a context with which the learner is at least partially familiar. Foreign language educators and applied linguists have struggled with this challenge for decades, coming up with various methodologies and approaches that attempt to address the many challenges associated with creating authentic contexts for learners, including the following:

- In notional–functional syllabi, vocabulary and grammatical points are presented in semantically coherent, related sets, with the understanding that this approach facilitates memorization and learning.
- In direct approaches, all language use in a classroom, including classroom decorations and management direction, is in the target language to provide learners with a sense of immersion in a meaning-rich context.
- In several approaches, role-plays are considered effective, because they require learners to consider contextual features when selecting linguistic structures and performing communicative functions.

In sum, contextualizing learning is a challenge for L2 educators, for which a variety of solutions have been developed. One approach that holds much promise, we believe, is a narrative approach in which language use is contextualized in stories and fictional worlds. Digital games are especially well suited to this approach, which we explain later.

5.2.2 Narratives and learning

We teach by telling stories. In other words, **narrative** is the means by which we transmit culture—for example, fairy tales, myths, and legends, but also films, novels, drama, and games. We also create situational and cultural context through narratives. In short, narrative is how we contextualize information. For example, at the level of conversation, narrative plays an important role in establishing mutual understanding and transmitting new information. When we come into the middle of a conversation, we sometimes do not understand what is being talked about, and so we might ask for the whole picture or the backstory. If we want to know even more, we need the history.[1] It is widely acknowledged that artists, writers, and storytellers create and transmit culture through narrative, and that narrative is how we interpret and understand human activity on a broader level as well—for example, history, law, and religion.

Some cognitive theories of learning (Anderson, 1977; Fauconnier & Turner, 2002; Lakoff & Johnson, 1980) argue that we cannot learn new information unless it is put in terms of frames and schemas that are at least partially recognizable. From this point of view, we learn best when we can situate our

---

[1]In some languages such as French, the word for history and story are the same (*l'histoire*). In English, it is easy to see that they are etymologically related.

knowledge and have a framework for new understandings. When some contextual features are familiar and others are not, we use the familiar ones to infer something about the others. Narratives, like stories, function as cognitive frameworks that contextualize new knowledge because some of the story elements are familiar. Narratives fit into genres, or culturally determined text types, about which readers (and learners) have expectations and understandings that they can use to learn new information and new stories.

Narrative-rich literature and film, of course, have been used throughout the history of L2 teaching. In good L2TL, learners are guided to go beyond simple reading to experience the narratives in relevant, meaningful ways. A narrative-informed approach has been proposed as an effective way to contextualize L2 learning (e.g., Hager, 2004; Shrum & Glisan, 2005). In this approach, learners experience a story and use contextual clues to predict and learn meaning. Focus is initially on whole understanding rather than on discrete vocabulary and grammar points. Literacy-based approaches (e.g., Allen, 2009; Allen & Paesani, 2010; Kern, 2000) also work with narratives, using the idea of situated learning and transformed practice (New London Group, 1996) to have students work with texts in meaningful ways and understand literacy as dynamic and individualized. Genre-based and awareness-focused approaches (see Reinhardt & Thorne, 2011) also use context as an organizing principle.

As mentioned earlier, digital games use narratives to contextualize game rules, creating an immersive in-game context. As discussed in Chapter 3, a player interacts with a game more actively than with other sorts of texts, such as books and movies. A game designer uses narratives, with characters, stories, and images, to contextualize game structures and, through these elements, is able to animate feedback mechanisms, allow for goal orienting, afford interaction, and teach players how to play the game. Narratives are, therefore, an important part of games. The fact that players are forced to interact with them is one reason that games are so motivating and immersive (see Chapter 6) as well as why they can function so well as learning environments.

5.2.3 Your reflections

1. Describe the strengths and drawbacks of the structural and functional views of language and their different understandings of the concept of *context*.
2. Consider the concepts of *context of situation* and *context of culture*. Think of your experiences learning an L2, particularly an event in which you had difficulty understanding or communicating something. In which area of context did your difficulties lie?
3. Think of your experiences teaching an L2. How do you make classroom experiences genuine and authentic for learners? How do you contextualize these experiences?
4. How do you use narratives to teach an L2, or have you used them to learn an L2 yourself? What are the challenges of teaching and learning with narratives?

5.3 GAMES AND NARRATIVES

Digital games are unique among media because of their interactive properties. Scholars in a variety of fields have studied them both as texts and as
practices. This dual nature of games, as things you both read (in a way) and
experience through play, has resulted in much debate in communication
studies, sociology, education, and cultural studies, the fields where digital
games have been studied most intensively. Some argue that digital games
are at their core collections of **rules**, designed to create emergent activities or to lead through a progression of activities (Juul, 2005), and that the
narratives in which games are contextualized are complementary, but not
entirely necessary, for play. Frasca (1999) noted that whereas games can be
seen as a series of choices and activities leading to further choices, true narratives involve sets of chained actions already predetermined by an author.
Although a reader may actively construct the fictional world around a narrative, the story has already been set in place and cannot be altered by the
reader. A completed game session may resemble a narrative, but a single
session is not the same thing as the game itself.

Simons (2007) noted that designing a game is equivalent to authoring a
narrative, but playing a game may be likened to reading or watching a narrative or to exploring alternative narratives. According to Neitzel (2005), the
computer-mediated quality of digital games results in a separation of seeing and
acting, and playing is a back-and-forth process of self-observation and continuous feedback. This interactive quality between action and representation, or
between what is represented and its representation, "forms the basis of every
narrative" (p. 231), including games. Carr (2006) noted that the analytic framework traditionally used for narratives—for example, narrator, what or who is
narrated, implied author, and implied reader—is only partially applicable to
games, because some of these roles do not exist in games. In addition, in
games, players can shift among these roles quite easily—one reason, she specu-
lates, why games can be highly engaging.

Calleja (2007) considered two perspectives on narrative: **designed narrative**, or the background fictional world that contextualizes game content, and
personal narrative, or the "player's interpretation of the gameplay experience" (p. 250). For a player to progress through a game, designers may require
that particular designed narratives be watched—for example, in the cut-scenes
of role-play games or interactive fiction, or they may allow them to be bypassed
or ignored, which is common with advanced players who may focus more on
rules and strategies (Juul, 2005). In *RU Emergency Response Unit* (Figure 5.1),
the designers have embedded a number of video clips and images related to
international aid work.

A personal narrative, in contrast, is what Juul (2005) termed *emergent
narrative*, or a player's story of what he or she experienced during a particular
gaming session. The personal narrative may include completing quests, interacting with other players, and fighting fictional characters, and for each player
it is different. For example, in *RU Emergency Response Unit*, the player decides

FIGURE 5.1 RU Emergency Response Unit This game contextualizes gameplay in global disaster narratives. Players must travel the world to assist in disaster aid activities. *Source*: Youda Games (2008).

how to manage and distribute various resources and personnel to manage aid services at a number of global natural disaster sites (Figure 5.2).

Calleja noted that personal narratives might heighten the affective dimensions of a game. For many players, they become more important than designed narratives, as they provide players with a strong sense of agency. It is the interaction between the two types of narratives that serves as "the locus of meaning making within designed environments" (2007, p. 252).

Designed narratives can be understood as providing the context-in-the-game, as they are placed in the game by the game developers to implement the game structure. Yet the designed context is not fully realized until it is played, that is, until a player creates his or her own personal narrative by playing it. Designed narratives may include linguistic and cultural content with which players may negotiate and construct meaning to create personal narratives. As discussed in Chapter 3, these interactions may occur with the game content, with others through and around the game, and about the game in extended, attendant discourses. In terms of context, it is therefore the context of play where personal narratives may emerge—that is, where, why, how, and with whom the game is played. These situational and cultural meanings arise from the socially and culturally interactive aspects of gameplay.

FIGURE 5.2 RU Emergency Response Unit *Source*: Youda Games (2008).

5.3.1 Your reflections

1. How do you think playing a game is similar to, and different from, experiencing other narrative forms, such as reading a novel or watching a film? Would you say that those experiences are also interactive?
2. What sorts of personal narratives do you have about playing games? If you have played a game, tell a story about your experience. If not, what other sorts of personal narratives do you have about other stories, such as those in novels, movies, or TV shows? How is your personal narrative intertwined with the story narrative?
3. Carr (2006) has noted that when players report their personal game narratives, they use *I* to refer to both their actual selves and their in-game characters (or avatars). What is the significance, if any, of this back-and-forth movement between the game narrative and the outside-the-game narrative?

5.4 CONTEXT IN GAME-INFORMED L2TL

The context of play is both situational and cultural, which should be taken into consideration in the design of any game-mediated L2TL environment. In-game designed narratives, as well as emergent personal narratives, can and should serve as resources for L2 learning. In game-enhanced L2TL, the narratives found in particular games and game genres can be aligned to curricular demands and learner needs. Units of instruction, lessons, and classroom activities can be built around games. Many games, especially adventure and role-play games, are rich in narratives that reflect a variety of cultural discourses useful for L2TL. Other game genres also contain applicable discourses and vocabulary. For example, city simulation games can be used for contextualized practice of city vocabulary or directions, and restaurant management games can be used for food and cooking vocabulary (see Appendix II). As a game-enhanced pedagogical framework, a literacy-focused, narrative approach that recognizes games as both texts and practices is useful (Reinhardt & Sykes, 2011). In this approach, learners design new narratives by exploring, examining, and extending game narratives and discourses.

When creating game-based L2TL environments, game designers should recognize that in-game narratives contextualize game rules and, at the same time, are made real in the context of play. These designed narratives should be relevant to learner and instructor needs, and they should also contextualize the target L2 items. L2 understanding is then achieved by using the language meaningfully to play the game. In other words, the player should have to use the L2 in meaningful ways to learn the gameplay rules and to play the game. Designed narratives, therefore, contextualize learning of both L2 discourses and game structures. Game-based L2TL applications may be comprehensive, as synthetic immersion environments, they may be focused on only a few notions, functions, and structures, or they may be contextualized in smaller, shorter narratives as casual or mini-games. L2TL-purposed games need not be as graphically rich and all-encompassing as a MMOG such as *World of Warcraft*, for example. The most successful games are popular because of their gameplay structures and narratives, not necessarily because of their technological sophistication.[2]

The design of game-based L2TL applications should also promote the designing of personal narratives and game-mediated interactions that complement L2TL activity outside the game. Personal narratives, for example, can be recorded in a gaming journal (see Section 2.6.1, Activity 2A) and used for extension activities. If the game does not afford social or cultural interactions or if it is not adaptable to L2TL classroom implementation, it will be neither commercially successful nor effective as a learning tool.

The notion that narratives contextualize game rules and structures but that the game is not realized until it is actually played has important implications for L2TL and for our understanding of language more broadly. Game developers recognize that it is not only the context-in-the-game, but also the context of play that makes a good game. A collection of game structures on its own may comprise a game, but only through the power of narrative, both designed and

---

[2]Although most gamers would agree with this statement, it is also true that many games are admired for their graphically rich and artful qualities, which may require advanced technologies. One may argue, however, that these graphics are actually part of a game's narrative aspects.

personal, are these structures realized as a game. In theoretical terms, structure has no meaning and, in fact, cannot exist without both an internal and an external functional context. Structure is thus realized through use. Foreign language educators and applied linguists should note that even though a curriculum, syllabus, unit, lesson, or activity may be well designed with contextualizing narratives and meaningful, relevant applications, it is the context of learning where the context-in-the-lesson is realized, so to speak, on both situational and cultural levels. The best-designed lessons can fail in implementation if they are not connected to learners' needs and lives.

5.4.1 Your reflections

1. Look at Appendix II: Guide to Game Types and Genres and think of digital games that you know of or have played. How might their content or their designed narratives correspond to the units commonly found in L2TL syllabi?
2. With some games, players sometimes ignore designed narratives after developing expertise. They focus instead on game rules and strategies. What does this mean for L2TL, if we wish learners to continue focusing on narratives?
3. Do you agree with the game-informed idea that narrative is a highly effective way to contextualize new knowledge? Besides narrative, what are other meta-cognitive functions involved in L2TL?

5.5 SUMMARY AND IMPLICATIONS

The following points summarize the main ideas of this chapter on context, with implications for transforming L2TL:

1. Structural approaches consider grammar the foundation of language. According to these approaches, language is modular. Although context may influence meaning, meaning exists independently of use.
2. Functional approaches consider context to be central to language meaning, and contextualized use as central to language learning. From a functional viewpoint, language has meaning only in its context of situation and, on a broader level, culture.
3. Narrative is a means by which we create and transmit culture. We learn, teach, and communicate through narratives because they provide cognitive frameworks for learning new information. Narrative-informed approaches to L2TL focus on the contextualizing power of narratives to develop L2 literacies.
4. Game design makes a primary distinction between game rules and structures and game narratives. Designers use narratives, which include characters, stories, and images, to contextualize game rules and structures. These narrative elements allow for goal orienting, afford interaction, and animate feedback mechanisms.
5. A designer places a designed narrative in the game to contextualize gameplay. This context-in-the-game is different from the context of play, which involves where, why, how, and with whom the game is played.

6. Personal narratives emerge from the context of play. They have situational and cultural meanings that arise from the socially and culturally interactive aspects of gameplay.

7. Designed and personal narratives can be used as resources for L2TL. In game-mediated L2TL, designed narratives can be aligned with curricular demands and learner needs. Narratives should be used to contextualize both targeted L2 use and game rules and structures, so that players have to learn the L2 in order to play the game.

5.6 A GAME-ENHANCED SCENARIO: *DESIGNING GAME NARRATIVES*

In consideration of the insights discussed in this chapter, we return to our learning scenario using a game-enhanced L2TL approach.

Ikegami-sensei became interested in games when she noticed that her student Peter tried using slang that she knew he did not learn from the course. When she asked him about it, he said that he learns slang from playing Japanese games and from online gamer forums. In one of his recent journal entries, he wrote from the perspective of his *Final Fantasy* game character, so that instead of the normal "Today I ate toast for breakfast," he wrote something like "Today I outwitted the leader of the cave tribe," which struck her as very creative. She did some research, and she found that many role-play games are quite story-like, so she thought she might offer some extra credit to students who tried to play a Japanese game. She thought about the basic way she learned to teach literature—to have students analyze characters, settings, and plot—and she tried to imagine the same framework for playing a game. She found an old worksheet with the framework and gave it to Peter and told him that he could tell her more about his game for extra credit by using this framework. His report was interesting, and she is now thinking about other ways she might use digital games for learning Japanese. She might ask her son to bring in his old PlayStation and some old games and set them up in the language lab.

Cindy is very interested in Peter's project, because some of her friends in Japan talk about playing games. She has played an online social networking game called *Poupee Girl* with her Japanese friends, and she is wondering if she could write a story about it for extra credit. Roberta also heard about Peter's report. She went to fanfiction.net, where she found over 12,000 fan fiction stories about *Final Fantasy*. She read some and became really interested, and she wondered if she could write fan fiction in Japanese. For his part, Peter is feeling proud of himself, and he is thinking about doing a double major in game design and Japanese.

5.6.1 Scenario questions

1. Think of a simulation, roleplay, or adventure digital game you have played. What narratives and discourses are in the game? How could these elements be used for an L2 learning activity? If you have not played such a digital game, consider a non-digital game you have played, such as a board game or a murder mystery roleplay.

2. What sort of extension activities could be done with the report that Peter produced about his game?
3. Do you think that working with game-mediated narratives can be as effective as working with more traditional narratives, as in novels or films? Why or why not?

5.7 GAME-MEDIATED APPLICATIONS

In this section, we offer three applications of concepts discussed in this chapter. Each is derived as an example of the general implementation frameworks we presented in the introductory chapter of this book. We first offer a description of the game-enhanced roleplay activity envisioned in the scenario. We follow with a framework for designed narratives in a game-based L2 learning environment, and then we offer final questions and ideas for game-informed reflections.

5.7.1 A game-enhanced L2 activity: *Designing narratives*

The objective of this activity is for L2 learners to develop digital L2 literacies by extending the designed and personal narratives they experienced while playing an adventure, action-adventure, roleplay, or interactive fiction game. Adventure and roleplay games are more linear than other genres. They usually have a plot, which makes them applicable to narrative-informed L2TL approaches. In the project, students complete activities during and after playing the game, and they use these resources to design new narratives through production, discussion, and presentation.

Procedures
1. Choose a game for the class to play, using Appendix II: Guide to Game Types and Genres and Appendix III: Guide to Evaluating Games as sources of ideas. Spend some time playing the game yourself and reviewing the activities, translating and customizing the activities as needed. Make sure the necessary computers and game copies are accessible.
2. Use a computer with a projector to demonstrate the game. For the demonstration, go through at least part of the tutorial or basic gameplay tasks, checking for comprehension and understanding. If possible, ask students to direct you and make choices for you as you play.
3. Have students play the game in groups of two or three. One student should be the mouse/keyboard controller, while the other(s) play(s) the role of note taker(s). Students can alternate roles during gameplay sessions if desired.
4. Allow students to play the game for one session with their only task being to learn the game and play it. Give the note takers the task of writing down what happens in the game as their group plays it, including at least five new vocabulary items.
5. For each subsequent play session, introduce a new activity, starting with the character descriptions (5A), adding setting descriptions (5B), and

finally adding the plot descriptions (5C) activities. Each can be on a new page, or groups can keep the descriptions in an ongoing journal.

6. After each session, hold a debriefing in which groups share their experiences. You can also require that groups turn in their descriptions at the end of each session.

7. Once groups have finished the game, have them complete the follow-up project (5D). The final project can be in a variety of formats, depending on student abilities and curricular demands—for example, a multipage prose story, a dialogue, or a script. The mode of the project can be a paper, presentation, or performance. Alternate modes requiring more preparation include a comic strip (e.g., with www.makebeliefscomix.com), a timeline (e.g., with www.timetoast.com), or a video (e.g., with sites such as www. xtranormal.com or movie-making software such as iMovie).

8. Provide students with the assessment rubrics you will use, based on the various aspects of the activities and final project. Include criteria as needed, for example, group participation; creativity; style and format; performance/presentation; and linguistic elements such as grammatical accuracy, vocabulary complexity, pronunciation, and so on.

Notes

- If necessary, provide students with the target language they need to interact with each other while playing the game.
- Individual students could complete the activities on their own, or the class could do the activities as a single group, with students taking turns as controllers.

ACTIVITY 5A

Designing narratives—Character descriptions

This activity should be completed for each of the in-game (non-player) characters that you encounter.

A. What is the character's name?
B. Describe his/her appearance.
C. Describe his/her personality.
D. Describe his/her role in the game (e.g., quest giver, enemy, shopkeeper).
E. How do you feel about this character? Why?

A. Name	B. Appearance	C. Personality	D. Role	E. Evaluation
1				
2				
(cont.)				

ACTIVITY 5B

Designing narratives—Setting descriptions

This activity should be completed for each of the settings or places in the game that you encounter.

A. What is the name of the place?
B. Describe its appearance. What does it look like?
C. What unique qualities does this place have?
D. What is the place for? What can you do here?
E. How do you feel about this place? Why?

A. Name	B. Appearance	C. Qualities	D. Function	E. Evaluation
1				
2				
(cont.)				

ACTIVITY 5C

Designing narratives—Plot descriptions

This activity should be completed after every game session. For this activity, you should record what actions happened during the game.

A. What happened during this session? What were the main points in the action?
B. Which characters were involved? How did your character develop?
C. What did you learn about the game narratives?
D. What do you think will happen next in the game?

Session	A. Plot points	B. Characters	C. Narratives	D. Predictions
1				
2				
3				
(cont.)				

ACTIVITY 5D

Designing narratives—Follow-up project

For this project, write an alternative or additional story using the characters and settings of the game. Your story can be a prequel, a parallel story, an alternate ending, or a sequel to the game. Use the plot description to make your story similar, but not too similar, to the plot of the game; in other words, it should be believable. Your instructor will provide guidelines for how long the story should be and what format it should have. To help you plan your story, use this framework.

Group Members:
Format:
Length:

1. What is the title of your story?

2. Who are the characters involved?

3. What are the settings of the story?

4. What happens in the story? Describe the plot.

5.7.2 Designing a game-based L2TL environment: Focus on context

As in previous chapters, this section focuses on the design of one specific element of the game, in this case, context. It should be used in conjunction with the content from the other sections you have worked on (e.g., goals, interaction, and feedback). In this section, we offer a framework that designers, instructors, and learners can use to think about context in the design of game-based L2TL environments (i.e., SIEs). Depending on the level of learner, the whole activity can be completed in the target language, or specific elements can be designated as "target language only."

Procedures
1. Prepare, modify, and translate the activity sheet as necessary.
2. In class, explain to the students that they will be helping design a digital game for language learning and will be focusing on context. This can be done in conjunction with the other design activities in other chapters or as its own process.
3. Explain the objectives of the activity: to develop a critical awareness about games, rethink context and narrative for language learning to be more effective, and design game narratives.
4. Have students complete the activities from Section 5.7.1 of this chapter so they have a better understanding of the structures of context and narratives in games.
5. Have learners work in groups to complete the game design activity.

CHAPTER 5   Game design activity: Design a digital game to learn [insert language]—Context

You have been given a grant to help build a digital game that helps students learn [insert language]. One step in the design process is coming up with the narratives that the game will have. As a group, design the narratives of your game by answering the following questions. Be sure to include as much detailed information as possible.

1. Basic Information
   a. What will you learn?
   b. What type of game is it (e.g., simulation, adventure)?
   c. What is the object of the game (what a player does to win)?
   d. What is the context of the game (setting, characters, etc.)?
2. Context
   a. **Plot**. Describe the context of the game in terms of what the game is about. If it is an adventure game, what are the major plot points?
   b. **Main character (avatar)**. Describe the choices the player has for the main character's name, appearance (including physique and clothing), personality, and talents or abilities.
   c. **In-game (non-player) characters**. Describe three or four characters in the game besides the player. Include their names, appearance, personalities, and roles.
   d. **Settings** (include name, appearance, unique qualities, and function when necessary).
      i. Describe the game world.
      ii. Describe the starting area for the player.
      iii. Describe one of the settings of the game.
3. **Map**. Draw a map or sketch of the whole game, the starting area, or one of the settings.
4. **Opening narrative**. Write out the opening narrative or scene. Include a script of the voice-over and a description of the images that the players will see when they start the game, before they begin to play.

5.7.3 Your game-informed reflections

A game-informed approach suggests a reconceptualization of context in the classroom. It is not embodied in one specific learning activity. Reflect on the chapter and write about and/or discuss the following topics:

1. Think about a particular class or course, and then reflect on your understanding of language, context, and narratives. Based on the chapter discussions, how might you reconceptualize them?
2. Consider a textbook you use or have used to teach, or one that you have used as a learner. What view of language does it reflect? What designed narratives does it present to learners? How does it support the creation of personal narratives by learners?

3. Consider the context-in-the-lesson of your own L2 teaching or learning, that is, the context that the textbook or lesson would have you imagine. How easy or difficult was it to teach or learn this context?

4. Consider the context of learning of your L2TL experiences. How has it been at odds with the context-in-the-lesson?

5. How could you incorporate game-informed notions of designed and personal narratives, context of play, and context-in-the-game into your own classroom, even without the use of digital games?

6. Action research is critical to furthering our understanding of narrative and context in digital games for language learning. What types of research projects would be most helpful? How would you investigate, for example, the usefulness of various kinds of designed narratives for L2TL?

CHAPTER **6**

Motivation
Engagement and flow

6.1 A SCENARIO: *KEEPING STUDENTS INTERESTED*

Mme. Smith

Mme. Smith is teaching a French course and really enjoys the students, her class, and the material. She is extremely enthusiastic, loves to be in the classroom, and always provides opportunities for her students to attend cultural events outside of class. There is not a more passionate, prepared, and enthusiastic teacher in the French program. Despite her efforts, Mme. Smith is facing some challenges. First, she is having trouble focusing her students on learning French for more than just a good grade. Even though she tries hard to motivate them, the default for students always seems to be the grade. For example, last week she put together a game-enhanced project that involved playing a cooking game to learn lexical items. This was followed by students preparing a report on regional styles of French cuisine. Although the students were successful with the activity, some did not really engage with it beyond what they needed to do to get As. She had hoped they would want to do more.

Second, the majority of Mme. Smith's students are not choosing to study French beyond beginning proficiency levels—about three-quarters do not plan to continue past the fourth semester. She encourages them to continue by pointing out the many benefits of advanced language study, the opportunities for study abroad, and the economic benefit advanced proficiency in French may have for their future careers. Nevertheless, students do not seem to want to continue.

The Students

Toward the end of the semester, Mme. Smith asks her students why they do not want to go on to fifth-semester study. She is curious about their motivations, and she hopes to use the information to improve retention rates.

Ruby believes that she has met her goal of getting As in all her French courses, and she does not want to risk getting a B in higher-level courses, which she heard were taught by tough professors. Layla tells Mme. Smith that she is not interested in continuing because she thinks she has the basics down and can put four semesters of French on her resumé. She believes that she has met her goal of taking French to help her land a good job. Reggie reports that he had not thought about continuing with French until the cooking activity, and he has been recently thinking about majoring in culinary arts with a minor in French, but he was not sure he wanted to take any literature courses at higher levels. He said he wished there were cooking and business courses taught in French.

6.1.1 Scenario Questions

1. Does this scenario resonate with you? Does it seem reflective of the beginning-intermediate sequence (often the first two years) in the foreign language classroom? Why or why not?
2. What are some factors in this scenario that are related to the motivation of the students? Do other contextual and social pressures contribute to this situation?
3. What role do grades play in this scenario? Is this dynamic common to most L2TL contexts?

This scenario presents a common situation in L2TL. Although the complex factors associated with motivation are difficult to isolate, they are often guided by the contextual, institutional, and cultural assumptions of students' learning environments, as is the case with Mme. Smith and her class. Although a game-mediated approach does not change or solve these constraints, the examination of motivation in digital games can help explain the tension educators often feel between the intense engagement of students with digital games and their lack of similar intensity when they are involved in school or other learning environments. Our hope is that by examining the engaging properties of digital games, educators develop a better understanding of motivation and are able to engage students in all educational contexts, not just game-enhanced ones.

6.2 MOTIVATION IN L2TL

The important role of motivation in L2TL and digital gameplay experiences is unmistakable, but the complex factors associated with it in both areas are numerous, intertwined, and difficult to tease apart. We can identify highly motivated language learners and learning activities that seem to motivate, yet engaging unmotivated learners is another story. It is not uncommon to hear educators, administrators, and parents lament students' lack of motivation toward studying. These complaints are sometimes accompanied by a comment or two about the hours students "waste" playing digital games or using popular media such as social networking sites and mobile applications. We do not deny the negative impacts that unproductive use of immersive technologies may have. However, as an alternative to considering all uses as wasteful, we propose that a more thorough understanding of motivation in L2TL and digital games will lead to informed decisions about their use and, as a result, allow educators to tap into their motivational power.

As a first step, we explore the parallels between motivation in L2TL and digital games. We then examine several models of motivation in L2TL, followed by an exploration of motivation in digital games through a focus on flow and engagement. Although the other chapters of this book can be read in any order, we highly recommend saving this chapter for last, as it requires background knowledge from the other five chapters. After exploring motivation in digital games, we conclude with implications for L2TL, a summary of main points, a new scenario, and ideas for teaching and research. As with other chapters, we encourage you to stop and ponder the questions for discussion and reflection throughout ("Your reflections").

6.2.1 Motivation models in L2TL

Motivation in L2TL is a hotly debated theoretical construct with a rich empirical history. In an attempt to operationalize the concept of motivation and understand how it impacts L2 acquisition, researchers have examined motivation as a predictive, preexisting variable that learners bring to the classroom, as well as something resulting from an activity. Whereas traditional approaches have conceptualized motivation as fixed, binary, and predetermined in nature, most researchers now acknowledge that motivation is dynamic, multifaceted, and just as often the result of, rather than the precondition of, an activity. More recent models, therefore, describe relationships among motivational factors and do not claim to be predictive. From a sociocultural perspective, motivation is not something that precedes or results from activity, but something that emerges with it.

The **integrative-instrumental orientation model** (Gardner & Lambert, 1972) is the longest standing, most discussed theory of motivation in L2 learning. In their model, Gardner and Lambert propose that a learner may be motivated by the desire to learn about, or integrate into, a new culture, whereas others may be motivated by the need to learn the L2 for instrumental reasons. *Integrative orientation* refers to the learner's desire to become proficient in the L2 to associate with the L2 community on a variety of levels. These include sensitivity to cultural concerns and even possible adoption of L2 community behaviors and values. *Instrumental orientation*, on the other hand, involves learning a language for the attainment of other goals. These goals may include getting a job, getting a raise, reading a specific article, or translating a document. A learner's integrative or instrumental orientation, combined with his or her perception toward the learning situation, determines motivation.

Although the concepts may be useful, the model is, of course, not perfect. Whereas some research has found integrative orientation to be more conducive to sustained success in L2 learning, in some cases, instrumental orientation proves to be a strong motivator (e.g., Gardner & MacIntyre, 1991; Lamb, 2004; Warden & Lin, 2000). For example, if only a few million people speak one's native language, learning another language may be the only way to travel internationally, find a high-paying job, or participate in popular world culture. As many expert English speakers around the world can explain very fluently, they have no desire to integrate into British or American society, but rather find English both relevant and beneficial for professional reasons. For many L2 learners, integration may not actually be feasible or possible, because of the biases and expectations of the target culture. For example, some English-speaking female learners of Japanese can find the adoption of honorifics marking gender to be incongruent with their beliefs and, as a result, never choose to fully integrate into Japanese cultural systems (Ishihara and Tarone, 2009). People study, and successfully learn, other languages for many reasons, not just two diametrically opposed ones. Moreover, there is no reason one cannot hold both integrative and instrumental orientations simultaneously, among other orientations. Finally, as any L2 learner knows, the reasons one decides to learn a language are not always those that continue to motivate through more advanced study. Over time, one's motivations change. As such, making predictions based on fixed, preexisting factors proves quite difficult.

In response to inadequacies of earlier models and advances in psychological research, leading L2 motivation researcher Zoltan Dörnyei (2001, 2005, 2009) proposed two useful, interrelated models: the **process model of learning motivation** and the **L2 motivational self system model**. Dörnyei's models do not claim to predict how motivation causes learning, but rather, they describe how motivational factors are interrelated in complex ways. His process model (2001) accommodates the notion that motivation is a dynamic process and can shift over time. A learner may begin an activity with a particular initial *choice motivation* but invests time and effort with *executive motivation* while completing the activity. Finally, the learner engages in *motivational retrospection*, reflecting on the process and reestablishing orientation toward new choices. Dörnyei's self system model (2005) captures the fact that motivation is multidimensional. The model is composed of three components: the *ideal L2 self*, the *ought-to L2 self*, and the *L2 experience*. The ideal L2 self refers to the L2 speaker whom an individual would like to become. For example, a learner might imagine himself at a coffee shop hanging out and interacting with native speaker friends. The ought-to L2 self refers to what an individual believes she ought or ought not to be. For example, if a learner believes she will not get into a good graduate program without being bilingual, learning the L2 is something she ought to do because it would lead to a positive outcome, whereas remaining monolingual would have a negative impact. The L2 experience refers to the environments in which the L2 learning is occurring—for example, the classroom, the teacher, peer group, and the curriculum—and their relationship to motivation. Any of these contextual features may impact, and be impacted by, the ideal and ought-to L2 selves of the learners and other factors involved.

The self system model shows the complex relationship between **intrinsic** factors, or motivational factors that seem to occur for their own sake, with their origin in the individual, and **extrinsic**, or external factors, which are related to the attainment of an external reward. This model shows how these factors are intertwined socio-contextual reasons for doing an activity, as well as the difficulty in predicting features as either causative or resultant. The distinction between *intrinsic* and *extrinsic*, referring to the source of one's motivation, can be problematic if both are understood as predictive, because this falls into the same trap as the integrative-instrumental model. Indeed, as anyone who has studied an L2 can confirm, motivations are quite complex and difficult to identify, and an initial extrinsic reason for learning an L2 can easily develop over time into something more intrinsic. Sometimes a classroom learning activity seems to motivate learners, even those who initially seemed unmotivated. This gives rise to a chicken-and-egg conundrum—which comes first, learner motivation or the motivating activity?

Further insight into the origin and role of motivation in L2 learning comes from concepts we have discussed throughout this book, especially in Chapter 2 and Chapter 4, related to sociocultural theory and the notions of the zone of proximal development (ZPD), scaffolding, and learner agency. From a socio-cultural theoretical perspective, the question of motivation being intrinsic or extrinsic misses the mark, because, in fact, all activity is socially mediated and originally external to individual learners (Lantolf & Thorne, 2006). From this perspective, learning, or more accurately development, occurs first through regulation by others, such as peers or experts, and then moves toward self-regulation by internalization and participation (Lave & Wenger, 1991). Learning happens only when the processes of mediation are sufficiently scaffolded and within a learner's ZPD, leading the learner toward self-regulation. Ultimately, this results in a sense of agency and the ability to realize one's goals, along with what we would recognize as motivation. From a sociocultural theoretic perspective, motivation is thus an epiphenomenon, or by-product of develop-ment, rather than a prerequisite or a result of learning. Motivation emerges from meaningful engagement with material, not from the material itself. As we explained in Chapter 2, this is how *goal orienting* in game-informed L2 learning activity, when meaningful choices are given to learners, can lead to successful learning. In games, these choices are exactly what lead to a sense of engage-ment and flow, which we discuss next.

In sum, several useful theories of motivation in L2 learning may inform the design of L2 learning environments, game-mediated or not. We know that learners may be motivated to learn an L2 for a variety of intrinsic and extrinsic reasons, but that these reasons may shift and develop over time. No learning activity is ever without a situated context that influences its effectiveness, and no learner comes to learning without a history. However, because the relationships among factors are dynamic and complex, it is difficult, if not impossible, to pin-point an exact cause-and-effect relationship between motivation and L2 learning.

6.2.2 Your reflections

1. What motivated you to learn and/or teach a second language? What motivates your students or other learners whom you know? What con-cepts discussed earlier might best describe your and their motivations?

2. In your L2TL experience, how has motivation been preexisting and predictive of learning (or not learning)?

3. In your experience, how has motivation resulted from a learning activity?

4. To use sociocultural theoretic terms, how has motivation been a by-product of engagement, whether or not the activity itself has been obviously motivating?

5. In your experience, has motivation not been simple cause-and-effect, but, rather, dynamic, complex, and nonlinear in causation? If so, in what way?

6.3 MOTIVATION: THE PLAYER AND THE GAME

Well-designed games motivate players in a number of ways. Although games often have a more captive and self-selected audience than foreign language classes do, there is no doubt that many games "hook" and motivate players with their designs. Motivation is a driving force for the economic success (or failure) of a digital game. If players decide to play and keep playing, the game company and designers make money. However, if players are not motivated, they do not continue and there is, therefore, less revenue. Thus, game designers are attuned to engaging players and keeping them in the game. They use a number of complex mechanisms to do so, several of which we have discussed in previous chapters, such as goal orientation, interactivity, and feedback mechanisms. Two key concepts on which these mechanisms rely are *engagement* and *flow*. Both are important features of a motivating play and/or learning environment.

6.3.1 Engagement and digital games

Engagement, primarily discussed as a theoretical concept within the field of learning, is the quality of an activity that maintains attention and investment by those participating in it.[1] Engagement is what motivates players to interact with digital games in intense ways for long periods of time (Gee, 2005; Prensky, 2006; Taylor, 2006) and is ultimately what game designers seek to encourage in their designs. Prensky (2001) identified 12 elements of games that engage players (see Figure 6.1).

Although not all of these features are present in every game, games that are the most played or most interesting tend to exhibit the majority of these characteristics. Prensky's characteristics of engagement are similar to those discussed by Salen and Zimmerman (2004) and to those central to this book, albeit the terminology and organization used by each is distinct.

In an ethnographic study of university students' interaction with the popular MMOG *World of Warcraft*, Browell (2007) found that learners were indeed engaged with a variety of activities and components of the game. Some of the

---

[1] Although many game designers note the importance of engagement with a game, in the game design field, researchers analyze various elements of engagement from a variety of theoretical perspectives. It is included here because of its prominence in the games and learning field.

- Games are a form of fun. That gives us enjoyment and pleasure.
- Games are a form of play. That gives us intense and passionate involvement.
- Games have rules. That gives us structure.
- Games have goals. That gives us motivation.
- Games are interactive. That gives us doing.
- Games have outcomes and feedback. That gives us learning.
- Games are adaptive. That gives us flow.
- Games have win states. That gives us ego gratification.
- Games have conflict/competition/challenge/opposition. That gives us adrenaline.
- Games have problem solving. That sparks our creativity.
- Games have interaction. That gives us social groups.
- Games have representation and story. That gives us emotion.

FIGURE 6.1 Elements of games that engage us *Source*: Prensky (2001, p. 106).

common findings cited for this level of engagement coincide with Prensky's principles. These include the socialization opportunities within the game space (i.e., social interaction); leveling up and improving one's character (i.e., goals, win states); high-quality, aesthetically pleasing immersive experience (i.e., narrative, representation); and persistence (i.e., outcomes, fun, goals, rules). Furthermore, Browell asserted that many of these principles, especially mentoring and collaborative practices, should be used in the development of new educational models at the university level.

One common misconception is that games are engaging only for a certain population of players (e.g., young, male, and antisocial). However, research has shown that this is not necessarily the case. In fact, a variety of types of gamers and populations enjoy different types of games or even engage in the same games differently (e.g., Prensky, 2001; Taylor, 2006). In a recent research review, Felicia (2011) confirmed the positive impact digital games have on learning via engagement and flow with and around the games. She highlighted "control, challenge, complexity, achievable and clear goals, hidden secrets, adaptation, debriefing, conflict, fantasy, mystery, and safety [and narrative]" as especially important aspects for increasing motivation in digital games (Felicia, 2011, n.p.).

In sum, the reasons for which a game is engaging are varied and complex. Most posit that it is a combination of various features in the game design itself that leads to player engagement, not a preexisting combination of attitudes or orientations. As we have noted in previous chapters, well-designed systems of goal orientation, interaction, feedback, and context are key features of an engaging game. Most important, engagement is a key prerequisite to a *flow* state, a place where motivation, activity, and learning potentially converge.

6.3.2 Flow and digital games

Throughout this book, we have intermittently mentioned the concept of **flow** in digital games (e.g., Chapter 4). In examining the parallels between motivation in L2TL and digital games, the concept of *flow*, originally proposed by the psychologist Mihaly Csikszentmihalyi (1990), is especially relevant for understanding players' experiences and their real-time motivation to continue playing. A flow state is "a particular state of mind in which a participant achieves a high degree of focus and enjoyment" (Salen & Zimmerman, 2004, p. 336). Flow is a rich and meaningful experience that can occur in work, play, or social contexts and is different for each individual. In essence, we can conceive of flow as the ultimate manifestation of motivation.

Game designers regularly point to flow as a key aspect of motivating gameplay experiences (Fullerton, 2008; Salen & Zimmerman, 2004). Salen and Zimmerman (2004, pp. 237–238) noted that the eight elements of Csikszentmihalyi's concept correlate to components of meaningful game design and provide a useful model for describing player motivation in digital games. They distinguish four of Csikszentmihalyi's characteristics as *prerequisites of flow* in digital games that are ultimately elements of the digital game itself:

1. A challenging activity
2. Clear goals
3. Clear feedback
4. The paradox of having control in an uncertain situation

Salen and Zimmerman make a strong case for considering how games become meaningful when they create or encourage flow states, and they highlight the place that challenge, goals, feedback, and perceived agency have as prerequisites of these states. First, an activity has to be challenging for a state of flow to result. In terms of game design, Fullerton (2008) discusses the need to maintain a balance between challenge and ability. If a player becomes frustrated because a game task is too challenging or bored because it is too easy, he or she will give up. Second, a player needs to know what the goal of the activity is. As discussed in Chapter 2, this quality is key not only to creating and maintaining flow, but also the learning that comes with it. If players have a sense of agency as they play, they are more likely to create and maintain flow. Third, a player must have adequate, discernable feedback to properly assess his or her capacity. As discussed in Chapter 4, knowing how one is doing while playing is key to being able to progress at the appropriate level, rate, and amount of challenge. Finally, good game design can lead to flow if it paradoxically leads the player to feel he or she has control in an uncertain situation, even without knowing for certain the outcome of the situation.

Salen and Zimmerman also describe four elements as *effects of flow*:

5. Merging of action and awareness
6. Intense concentration
7. Loss of self-consciousness
8. Transformation of time

First, when in a state of flow, a player feels that action and awareness have merged and becomes unaware of himself or herself as separate from the action. In sports, this is sometimes called being "in the zone," when the body is so fully engaged in an activity that the game and the player seem unified, and performance is at its peak. A second effect of flow is total concentration, whereby the player has complete focus on the task at hand. Concentration is necessary if one is to meet a true challenge completely—frustration and boredom are distracting. A third effect is the loss of self-consciousness, whereby the player becomes part of the system. Similar to the merging of action and awareness, this is the result of concentration and focus. The fourth effect, whereby time is transformed, results when consciousness of the self is lost.

Ultimately, a sustained flow state can result in what can seem like effortless learning. From an L2TL perspective, this means learning is optimized when learners have sufficient challenge, clear goals, meaningful feedback, and a sense of agency in a learning activity. It is perhaps in these un-self-conscious moments, when awareness is heightened, that language learning flows, so to speak, as easily as when a player is fully engaged in a game.

6.3.3 Your reflections

1. Do you see additional parallels between the L2 motivation models discussed in Section 6.2 and the concepts of engagement and flow mentioned here? If so, what are they?
2. How does the concept of engagement relate to your L2TL experiences? In your opinion, what keeps learners engaged in learning?
3. Have you ever experienced flow while intensely engaged in an activity? How would you describe it? Have you experienced it learning or using your L2? What do you think contributed to this sense?
4. Based on the previous discussion, which game elements are the most critical when considering motivation in digital games?

6.4 SUMMARY AND IMPLICATIONS

The following points summarize the main ideas of this chapter on motivation, with implications for transformed L2TL:

1. Traditional psychological models of motivation view it as an attitudinal quality preexisting in individual learners that has a causative relationship to learning. More recent models view motivation as more dynamic, multifaceted, and less predetermined in nature, as much a result of learning as a cause of it. Recent models are, therefore, more descriptive than predictive in scope.
2. The traditional integrative-instrumental model highlights students' functional reasons for learning an L2. Recent research shows that there are more than two basic orientations towards L2 learning, and that integrative and instrumental orientations are not necessarily mutually exclusive.

3. The process model of learning motivation views motivation as a dynamic and shifting process that involves choice and retrospection.

4. The L2 motivational self system model recognizes the complex, inter-twined relationships among an L2 learner's ideal self, ought-to self, and L2 experience.

5. Extrinsic and intrinsic features may be useful for identifying various sources of motivation, but the labels may be misleading if they are seen as dichotomous and predictive.

6. Sociocultural theory views motivation as a by-product of development and engagement in a learner's ZPD, rather than as a cause or effect of learning.

7. Motivating designs generate player motivation in digital games. Ultimately, the designer must create a game players want to start playing and keep playing.

8. A sense of engagement emerges when players are invested and participating fully in a game. Well-designed systems of goal orientation, interaction, feedback, and context are key features of an engaging game. Engagement is a key prerequisite to a flow state.

9. Flow is a fundamental concept for game design and player motivation. It focuses on the mental state of the player that emerges from a meaningful play experience. Researchers study the prerequisites to flow and the effects of flow. Language learning may be optimized when learners experience flow states.

6.5 A GAME-ENHANCED SCENARIO: *GETTING MOTIVATED TO LEARN FRENCH*

Mme. Smith takes Reggie, Layla, and Ruby to lunch after the semester is over to get a better idea of what she could do to motivate them to continue taking French courses. Reggie starts joking about how he worries that he is now addicted to the cooking game they played in class, and he is wondering if there are other similar games he could play. The students then engage in a lively discussion about their favorite games and why they like them. Layla really likes social networking games because she gets to compete with her friends and be part of a larger community of players. Ruby counters that she really does not like digital games, but she wonders if they would be more interesting in French. As she listens, Mme. Smith realizes that many of the digital games her students are talking about may be highly engaging for them and may even motivate them to continue learning French.

Mme. Smith decides to play some social networking games over the summer and gets involved in a Francophone community playing *Cityville*, chatting with some and even friending some players to be online neighbors. She decides to build her fifth-semester course in the fall around the idea of motivation and self-reflection, using portfolios as an authentic assessment instrument. She builds the syllabus around popular topics and technologies in current-day France and includes a unit on social network gaming. This unit entails gameplay for the students in French; analysis of a few websites created by player communities; and cultural analysis of game culture in France, based on some interesting news stories on the growing game industry there. As a final project, she has students choose a digital game or other technology and write a review of it from the perspective of a French learner. In the reviews, she asks students to reflect on why they thought the technology was, or was not, a good way to learn French.

She implements the course, and the results are positive. Eight of the ten students chose to review a game. Six students wrote how they met several French speakers online through their games, and how they felt as if they were part of a community. One wrote that although she did not like games when she started the class, she liked that some fellow players did not know she was not French, and how that gave her a different sense of who she was, or could be, in a French world. Another student, who was already a hardcore gamer, talked about how he played *Diablo III* in French and encountered "griefing" in French, the practice in online multiplayer games of complaining and being difficult in group play. It was full of satire and especially complex French for a fifth-semester student. Another wrote how she feared she did poorly in her other classes because she would lose track of time while playing *Cityville*. Reggie, who decided to take the class after all, became friends with a few players who were studying to be chefs and is learning about the French system of culinary training from them. For his final project, he created a proposal for an online pâtisserie management game.

Overall, Mme. Smith was impressed and is working to include digital games in the sixth-semester course she is teaching in the spring. She is happy to see Layla on the class list for the spring and plans to send Ruby a message about the new syllabus.

6.5.1 Scenario questions

1. What is your reaction to the game-enhanced scenario? How might it have been done better? What would have made it worse?
2. What approach is the instructor using? What are its strengths and weaknesses? Have you done similar activities with students? Have you done them as a learner?
3. What aspects of the motivational models do you see in the students' behaviors? How did Mme. Smith's syllabus acknowledge different motivations?
4. How could you apply a similar unit to your L2TL context? What would be the benefits? What would be the challenges?

6.6 GAME-MEDIATED APPLICATIONS

In this section, we offer three applications of the concepts surrounding motivation from this chapter. Each is derived as a specific example of the general implementation model from the book: game-enhanced, game-based, and game-informed L2TL. We first present a game-enhanced activity focusing on motivation in vernacular games. We then present a template for game design and motivation in a game-based environment and then offer final questions and ideas for game-informed reflections.

6.6.1 A game-enhanced activity: Thinking about motivation

The objective of this activity is for L2 learners to develop digital L2 literacies, especially game literacy, by reviewing a game with which they are relatively familiar. The students are directed to reflect on how their games motivate and engage players, and to relate this to language learning activity.

Procedures

1. Have groups of students work with a game they know. Students should be relatively familiar with the game they are reviewing.
2. Go over the concepts of flow and engagement with the students, using the information in Section 6.3 as necessary. Ask them questions such as the following:
   a. What makes a movie, TV show, or book engaging (interesting) to you? What makes it boring?
   b. Have you ever lost yourself in a movie, show, or book? Why? What happens when you do?
   c. What helps you concentrate when you are trying to do something challenging?
   d. Would you rather do something easy and boring or something challenging and engaging? Explain your response.
   e. What makes a game interesting or boring?
3. Tell students they are going to review a game using the concepts of flow and engagement, and then think about how these concepts relate to their experiences learning the L2. Present the activities for students to complete.
4. After students have completed the activities, discuss their answers as a class.

Notes

- For lower-level students, the class may complete the assignment together with the same game.
- You may assign a follow-up assignment for the activities, such as a reflective writing or a presentation.

ACTIVITY 6A

Thinking about flow in games and learning (insert language here)

Part 1. Evaluate your game based on the concept of flow. Discuss each element with your group. How important do you think each is for a game to be considered good?

Element of flow:	How much do you think
1. The player stops being aware of himself or herself as separate from the action.	3 (very much) – 2 (so-so) – 1 (not much at all)
2. The player has complete focus on the task at hand.	3 (very much) – 2 (so-so) – 1 (not much at all)
3. The player becomes part of the system.	3 (very much) – 2 (so-so) – 1 (not much at all)
4. The player loses track of time because of complete involvement.	3 (very much) – 2 (so-so) – 1 (not much at all)
5. The player finds the activity not too hard, but not too easy either.	3 (very much) – 2 (so-so) – 1 (not much at all)
6. The player knows what the goal of the activity is.	3 (very much) – 2 (so-so) – 1 (not much at all)
7. The player is provided adequate feedback to properly assess his or her capacity.	3 (very much) – 2 (so-so) – 1 (not much at all)
8. The player feels he or she has control and choice, even though he or she does not know the outcome of the choice.	3 (very much) – 2 (so-so) – 1 (not much at all)

Part 2. Think about the concept of *flow* in terms of how you are learning (insert language here). Answer the following questions:

1. Have you ever forgotten that you are using the L2, even when you are using it? Why?
2. Which kind of L2 learning activities do you find most or least enjoyable? Why?
3. Do you think you could ever be mistaken for a native speaker of the L2? Why or why not?
4. What happens if an L2 learning activity is too hard? What if it is too easy?
5. What happens if you do not know why you are doing a particular L2 learning activity?
6. How do you feel if you do not know when you have made a mistake in the L2? How do you prefer to find out?
7. How do you feel if someone praises your use of the L2? Why would the person do this?

ACTIVITY 6B

Thinking about engagement in games and learning (insert language here)

Part 1. Evaluate your game based on the concept of *engagement* and complete the chart as a group. Discuss how important you think each principle is for a game to be considered good. After you complete the chart as a group, discuss your evaluations as a class.

How much do you think . . .	
1. the game gives you enjoyment	3 (very much) – 2 (so-so) – 1 (not much at all)
2. the game's rules are not too complicated	3 (very much) – 2 (so-so) – 1 (not much at all)

How much do you think . . .	
3. you can figure out the object of the game	3 (very much) – 2 (so-so) – 1 (not much at all)
4. the game is interactive	3 (very much) – 2 (so-so) – 1 (not much at all)
5. the game provides you with feedback as you play it	3 (very much) – 2 (so-so) – 1 (not much at all)
6. the game adapts to you as you play	3 (very much) – 2 (so-so) – 1 (not much at all)
7. the game praises you when you win	3 (very much) – 2 (so-so) – 1 (not much at all)
8. the game has different amounts of competition, challenge, and opposition	3 (very much) – 2 (so-so) – 1 (not much at all)
9. the game has elements of problem solving	3 (very much) – 2 (so-so) – 1 (not much at all)
10. the game is fun to play as a group	3 (very much) – 2 (so-so) – 1 (not much at all)
11. the game has interesting narratives and stories	3 (very much) – 2 (so-so) – 1 (not much at all)

Part 2. Think about the concept of *engagement* in terms of how you are learning (insert language here). Answer the following questions:

1. How important is it that you enjoy learning the L2?
2. How complicated do you think the rules of L2 grammar and usage are? How do you deal with complicated rules?
3. Do you always know the purpose of an L2 learning activity? What happens if you do not?
4. What kinds of L2 learning activities are interactive? Which are not?
5. What kinds of feedback do you like to get from your instructor? What kinds do you not like?
6. What happens if an L2 learning activity is too hard or easy?
7. Do you like to know if you have used the L2 correctly? Why?
8. How much do you like competing or collaborating with other students? Why or why not?
9. How much do you like figuring out rules and facts about the L2 language and culture? Why or why not? Would you rather just be told about them?
10. How important is it to use the L2 with other people? Why?
11. How much do you like hearing stories in the L2? Why or why not?
12. In sum, what engages you in learning the L2?

6.6.2 Designing a game-based L2TL environment: Focus on motivation

In this section focused on game-based environments, you will take what you have done in other chapters and apply considerations of motivation. This chapter's game design activity should be used in conjunction with the content from the other sections you have worked on to make the most of the overall game system: goals, interaction, feedback, and context. In this section, we offer guidelines that designers, instructors, and learners can use to think specifically about motivation in the design of game-based L2TL environments (i.e., SIEs). Depending on the level of the learners, the whole activity can be completed in the target language or specific elements can be designated as "target language only."

Procedures

1. Prepare, modify, and translate the activity sheet as necessary.
2. In class, explain to the students that they will be helping improve the design of a digital game for language learning and will be focusing on motivation. This is most effective when done in conjunction with the other game design activities from other chapters.
3. Explain the objectives of the activity: to develop a critical awareness about games, rethink motivation for language learning to be more effective, and design target language mechanisms to increase motivation for playing the SIE.
4. Have students complete the activity in Section 6.6.1 so they better understand the concepts of flow and engagement in digital games.
5. Have learners work in groups to complete the activity.

CHAPTER 6 Game design activity: Design a digital game to learn [insert language]—Motivation

You have been given a grant to build a digital game that helps students learn [insert language]. One step in the design process is ensuring that players are motivated to start playing and keep playing. Examine the other design activities you have done and critique them in view of the elements of flow and principles of engagement. For each aspect, think about the ways in which you could modify your game design to increase player motivation. Be sure to include as many details as possible.

1. Basic Information
   a. Intended Learning Objectives:
   b. Genre of the Game:
   c. Object of Game:
   d. Context of the Game (setting, characters, etc.):
2. **Flow** (See Section 6.3 for additional information on each element.)
   a. **Prerequisites of flow**. How does your game offer each of these elements? Which do you think is the most challenging to create? Why?
   b. **Effects of flow**. How does your game promote these elements? In which parts of your game do you think players will experience these effects?
3. **Engagement**: Examine each of Prensky's principles of engagement. How well do you think your game addresses each of the 12 elements? Where might your game need adjustment?
4. **Reflection**. How does your game motivate players to start playing and keep playing?

6.6.3 Your game-informed reflections

A game-informed approach suggests an integrative approach to motivation that takes advantage of the interconnectivity of L2TL. It is not embodied in one specific learning activity. Reflect on the chapter and write about and/or discuss the following topics:

1. Think about a particular course or class you have taught or taken. How motivated were the learners? Where does their motivation seem to fit into each of the L2TL motivational models discussed? How could you use a game-informed approach to impact this motivation? What sorts of game-mediated activities could increase motivation in students?

2. In this chapter, we saw how digital game systems create flow states to increase motivation in players. How is this complex system similar to, and different from, equivalent systems in L2TL, for example, in the design of learning activities, syllabi, or pedagogical approaches?

3. How could the principles of engagement presented by Prensky be applied to the design and implementation of L2TL environments?

4. Action research is critical to furthering our understanding of motivation in digital games for language learning. What types of research projects would be most helpful? How would you investigate, for example, the impact of digital game-mediated learning activities on L2 learning motivation or the application of game-informed principles of motivation (flow and engagement) on L2TL?

CHAPTER 7

Endgame
The future of digital games and L2TL

In this concluding chapter, we first review the main premises of each of the main chapters—goals, interaction, feedback, context, and motivation—and draw connections across chapters, with the goal of conceptual synthesis. We then highlight three considerations for our continued exploration of game-mediated L2TL:

- Games are complex, integrated systems.
- Player and learner agency are key.
- Games promote learning to play, rather than playing to learn (Arnseth, 2006).

This is followed by a discussion of the future of game-mediated L2TL and sample summary activities for game-enhanced and game-based scenarios.

7.1 FROM PARALLELS TO CONNECTIONS

In this section, we review key concepts presented in each chapter of the book, starting with parallels between concepts from digital game design and those from L2TL. We then focus on how each concept relates to concepts in other chapters. We invite readers to consider these parallels and connections, and to make their own.

7.1.1 Goals: Learning tasks and goal orientation

As discussed in Chapter 2, there are several notable parallels between how digital games are designed and the concepts of goal, task, and activity in L2TL. For example, goal orientation is a critical component of both digital game and

L2 learning task design. In comparison to some L2 learning tasks, however, game tasks are usually:

- Fundamentally player driven, as opposed to instruction-driven.
- Dynamic and continually negotiated, as opposed to static and unchangeable.
- Ongoing and incremental, as opposed to isolated and disconnected.
- Partially emergent, as opposed to entirely predetermined.

In game design, task choices are predetermined by the game designer but are authenticated by the player through perceived agency. Designers must pay special attention to the type of task presented to players, the level of task difficulty, the amount of perceived choice the task offers, and how relevant the task outcome seems. Furthermore, the delivery of feedback at just the right time allows for successful (or unsuccessful) task completion and goal achievement. Players become frustrated if goals are unclear or too difficult and bored if goals are too easy or repetitive. Without perceived agency, there is no motivation to continue playing the game. Goals should always be apparent and, at the same time, present a doable challenge, enabling a sense of flow. Salen and Zimmerman (2004, p. 338) describe this connection:

> The goals, challenge, and uncertainty of a game provide the larger context within which choices are *integrated* and become meaningful. This is not to say that meaningful play is the same thing as flow. Flow is a state of mind and meaningful play is an approach to game design. But, when it comes to games, the two are closely intertwined.

Ultimately, designers of meaningful L2 learning experiences can glean a great deal from this notion. When provided with doable challenges, integrated choices, and a sense of perceived agency in L2 learning tasks, L2 learners may experience a flow state, enabling them to persist through the difficulties often associated with continued language study. These tasks balance learner-driven with instruction-driven needs. In essence, the theory of learning behind game-mediated task design offers us a way to see goal orienting as a process, rather than a static condition, that can strengthen learner motivation.

7.1.2 Interaction: With, through, and about digital games

In Chapter 3, we discussed how game-mediated L2 learning should incorporate learner interactions with, through, and about the game being played. Interactions *with* the game can focus on the designed narratives or context-in-the-game, specifically the linguistic, socio-pragmatic, and cultural elements found there. A learning activity, for example, might focus on meaningful interaction with the new L2 vocabulary needed to play a particular game successfully. Interactions *through* or *around* the game are with other players, learning to play and playing the game. These interactions provide opportunities for the interpersonal use of the L2. Finally, interactions *about* the game are important, because they allow players to connect the designed and emergent narratives with broader, real-world contexts. Interactions can be in or outside the game environment itself, and tasks can be designed to promote all three types simultaneously.

From a design standpoint, games can promote *cognitive, functional, explicit,* and *cultural* interactivity. Depending on learner and instructional needs, game-enhanced L2TL activities should use games that promote these interactivities, and game-based applications should be designed with them in mind as well. Each type of interactivity with the game contributes to the player's motivation to keep playing and the potential for reaching flow states. Cognitive interactivity is promoted through an immersive, multimodal gameplay experience, with graphics, sounds, music, and narratives. This interaction helps highlight feedback mechanisms and creates the sensory immersion that is key to a flow experience. Functional interactivity is a matter of seamless, ergonomic, and nearly invisible interface design. It helps limit frustration and keeps attention on the gameplay itself, as opposed to how to play it. If the interface is not clear, the player quickly becomes frustrated and may stop playing. In other words, a poor interface design can prevent a sense of flow by consistently reminding players they are doing something, as opposed to experiencing something. Explicit interactivity develops by offering players choices and decisions to make, which leads to a sense of agency. If choice outcomes are not discernable and integrated, however, they do not lead to engagement. Explicitly interactive game designs also afford social interaction by promoting collaboration and competition among players in various ways. Finally, a culturally interactive game promotes the development of attendant discourses and various social practices in player communities.

7.1.3 Feedback: Real-time, individualized, and instructional

Feedback, discussed in Chapter 4, is closely tied with goal orientation, context, and motivation in digital games, and it has noteworthy parallels in the L2TL concepts of instructional feedback, scaffolding, and the sociocultural theoretical concept of the zone of proximal development (ZPD). To be effective, feedback must complement tasks by being provided in just the right amount, at just the right time, and in just the right way. Feedback helps mediate task difficulty. A task with too much feedback is boring; yet, the same task with few resources may result in a challenge too difficult to overcome. Similarly, an extremely difficult task with meaningful, timely feedback can create a highly engaging experience that motivates the player to keep playing. When the right piece of feedback is delivered at the right time, it has a strong motivational impact on the player:

> To improve gameplay [motivation to keep playing], a good designer must be able to evaluate how quickly or slowly the game is progressing, understand if there are patterns to growth or contraction in the system caused by reinforcing [feedback] loops, and know when and how to apply a balancing factor. (Fullerton, 2008, p. 139)

Because it is difficult to predict the progress rate of each potential player, game designers incorporate multiple kinds of feedback, providing players with an array of customizable resources. As explained in Chapter 4, L2TL has much to gain from understanding the individualized, instructional, just-in-time feedback systems found in digital games. By using meaningful, adaptive feedback systems for formative assessment in L2TL, instead of relying on high-stakes, after-the-fact, summative assessment, we may not only improve learner motivation, but also gain a better understanding of L2 development processes.

7.1.4 Context: The role of narrative

Context (Chapter 5) situates gameplay experiences in the form of designed narratives, or context-in-the game, and personal narratives, which emerge in the context of play. Critical to our understanding of these concepts is the fundamental role of context for understanding the meaning of language. From a functional viewpoint, language has meaning only in its context of situation and associated culture. In a similar way, game designers use designed narratives, including characters, stories, and images, to contextualize game rules and structures. These narrative elements allow for goal orienting, afford interaction, and animate feedback mechanisms. Without these contextualizing narratives, game rules and structures can seem disconnected and irrelevant to a player. Designed narratives both instruct and motivate players.

These narratives also combine with the personal narratives players create as they experience a game. Meaningful gameplay experiences thus emerge from the combination of the context-in-the-game and the context of play. In the same way, an L2 learning experience has the potential to be meaningful. A learner experiences designed narratives as part of a lesson, and personal narratives emerge in the context of learning. When these designed narratives contextualize L2 rules and structures, there is potential for learning, but outside of a narrative, L2 rules and structures are less relevant. Meaningful learning happens when the designed narratives of a lesson combine with the personal narratives of learners. In game-mediated L2TL, both in-game and out-of-game linguistic and cultural narratives should be used to contextualize both targeted L2 use and game rules and structures, so that players have to learn the L2 in order to play the game. Furthermore, the personal, situated narratives that emerge from the gameplay experience itself can be used as resources for extended learning and literacy development.

7.1.5 Motivation: Engagement and flow

Motivation is what keeps players playing and learners learning. As we discussed in Chapter 6, several models are popular in L2TL. Whereas traditional models are predictive in scope, current models are descriptive, and they conceptualize motivation as dynamic, multifaceted, and not easily reduced to cause and effect. Learners may be motivated to learn an L2 for a variety of intrinsic and extrinsic reasons, but these reasons may shift and develop over time. Good digital games are especially successful at keeping players motivated to continue playing, through provision of interesting tasks, player choices, interaction opportunities, scaffolded resources, instructional feedback, and meaningful narratives. If a game does not provide these elements, it fails to engage players. If the right prerequisites are met, a flow state may result, which may optimize the learning experience.

7.1.6 Your reflections

1. How strong do you think the parallels we set forward are? Can you see any other parallels between digital game design or gameplay and L2TL?
2. Of the five areas summarized in this section, which seems to be the most critical for L2TL? Why?
3. See if you can make some predictions about how each of these five areas connects to the others. Create a mind map or other diagram to represent as many connections as possible.

7.2 CRITICAL CONSIDERATIONS

Throughout the volume, we have touched on three underlying considerations that are critical for understanding the potential of game-mediated L2TL. First, games are complex, integrated systems, comprised of many interrelated elements. Second, games work because players have agency in playing them, whether real or illusory. Third, games are designed so that players learn the rules, structures, and designed narratives in order to play the game, not the other way around. In contrast, many educational games, digital or conventional, place the learning of particular content as the goal, and playing as the means to get there. Predictably, many educational games fail for this reason, as players see quickly through the ruse. This understanding is key to designing effective game-mediated L2TL experiences.

7.2.1 Parts of a system

In each chapter, we have attempted to highlight the parallels between various components of digital games and L2TL by isolating different focus points—goals, interaction, feedback, context, and motivation. While we recognize the value of isolating each for discussion purposes, we must also remain cognizant that these elements have a symbiotic relationship in digital games. Ultimately, they function as components of a complex, integrated system. For example, the amount and delivery of feedback are essential for providing a player with a sense of choice. In addition, in-game tasks must be contextualized in designed narratives, and interactions with, through, and about the game should foster personal narratives. Schell (2008) discusses the interplay of each of these elements in creating a balanced (i.e., positive) play experience. In doing so, he presents 12 balance types to consider when combining game elements (Table 7.1).

Without successful balance of all of the parts, the system can be thrown off-kilter, resulting in a game that is not enjoyable. L2TL is no different. We are able to isolate various components of language learning but cannot ignore the combined effect of all. Ecological approaches to L2TL

Table 7.1 Balance Types in Game Design

Balance Type	Description
Fairness	Fairness creates a balance between a player's resources and the forces working against him or her in a game. This can be achieved through symmetrical games (i.e., all players have the same resources) or careful delivery of resources in asymmetrical games.
Challenge vs. success	A game cannot be too easy or too difficult. The balance between success and failure is critical to making this happen. Means to achieve this balance include, for example, increased difficulty with success, speed of play, various layers of challenge, and player choice in the difficulty level.
Meaningful choices	Choices should be meaningful and have a direct impact on the outcome of the game. This requires a careful balance between the number and type of choices given and their direct impact. *Triangularity* can help achieve this balance (i.e., low-risk choices equal lower rewards, whereas high-risk choices result in higher rewards).
Skill vs. chance	There must be a careful balance between what happens to a player as a result of chance and as a result of his or her own abilities. This balance is highly dependent on individual play styles and player preferences.
Head vs. hands	There must also be a balance between the physical skills needed to play a game ("hands") and the thinking that is needed ("head"). This is distinct for different types of games. For example, a driving game might have more hands than head and an adventure game more head than hands.
Competition vs. cooperation	In a digital game, there must be balance between the amount of competition and cooperation. Team competition represents a strong example of balance between the two, as players cooperate with their team members but are united in competition against opponents.
Short vs. long	Designers need to be cautious of the length of gameplay. A game that is too short does not provide a meaningful experience for the players, whereas a game that is too long can become boring or too excessive in the time it requires to play.
Rewards vs. punishment	Tied to the balance of challenge and success, a game must also provide a balance between rewards (positive things given to the player) and punishments (things that happen to a player that often create challenge). Common rewards include praise, points, skills, gateways, powers, and resources. Common punishments include shaming, loss of points, terminated play, and removal of powers.
Freedom vs. controlled experience	A careful balance of what players can control and what is controlled by the game itself is necessary. Too much player control can be uninteresting and not enough control can be too challenging.
Simple vs. complex	A good game should be "simplistically complex." In other words, the simplicity makes the gameplay experience clear and enjoyable to play and the complexity makes it interesting, but not too confusing.
Detail vs. imagination	A designer has to make choices about how much detail to include and how much to give over to the player's imagination. Some ways to achieve this balance include detailing only what can be detailed well, giving details that can spark imagination, and not providing details about the familiar.

Source: Schell (2008).

(Larsen-Freeman & Cameron, 2008; van Lier, 2004) recognize the dynamic and systemic nature of this balance. All elements of a learning and teaching ecology are interconnected and interdependent. When one element is out of balance, the others falter. Incorporating a game into an L2TL learning environment means adding another complex element to the balance, one that has its own balance as a self-contained game but still requires integration into a larger system. We encourage researchers and practitioners to consider digital gaming, learning, and teaching as whole, integrated systems individually, and when combined, as a larger, even more complex system, greater than the sum of its parts.

7.2.2 Player and learner agency

In addition to seeing games as systems, it is critical to remember the central role of the player in the system. Player agency must be fostered and recognized as a crucial element of an activity (see Chapter 2), even as others design the structure of the activity. In activity design, this flexible structure allows for player choice with discernable outcomes, while providing direction and guidance. Individualized and timely feedback systems contribute to the sense of agency. This tension between the need to promote player agency and the need for outcomes to be at least partially predictable is at the heart of the definition of a game. In order to remain motivated to keep playing, players must know what they are doing and believe that they have choice in doing it.

In L2TL contexts, learners who do not feel a sense of agency risk becoming disenfranchised from the learning experience. Learning an L2 requires taking risks and experimenting with the new language, and if learners haven't had opportunities to develop autonomy, they will not feel comfortable taking the initiative to try. When every choice in an L2 classroom is met with judgmental evaluation, learners are more likely to shut down the next time they are offered choices. When measured risk taking and low-stakes failure are promoted, and feedback is targeted at just the right time, level, and amount, learners are more likely to persevere and develop autonomy.

7.2.3 Playing to learn vs. learning to play

In our consideration of game-mediated L2TL, we find Arnseth's (2006) distinction between *playing to learn* (i.e., players complete tasks in order to learn something important) and *learning to play* (i.e., the play experience itself is the motivation for players to learn something) to be noteworthy. We take the learning-to-play perspective, which emphasizes that digital games are not only valuable as a means to an end, but are the end itself—in learners' minds, they are learning something in order to play a game, not playing the game in order to learn something. In other words, they are players first, and learners second. This perspective should inform the design of both game-enhanced L2TL and game-based L2TL environments, and it corrects the misconception that game-based environments are somehow superior (for further discussion, see Chapter 1, also Reinhardt & Sykes, 2012), because they are purposefully designed for L2TL. From a learning-to-play perspective, the learning that happens as part of gameplay is at the core of the learning process and should be integrated with curricular goals, and not be seen as a means to the end of learning content.

7.2.4 Your reflections

1. Revisit your answer to question 3 in Section 7.1.6. Do your predictions reflect what you read here? Could you add to your diagram or mind map?
2. Select one of the games discussed throughout the book (see the games list on page 152 for a review). First, draw an image that reflects the many distinct parts of the system of the game you selected. Then, imagine ways in which this system might parallel L2TL. How would your drawing be the same when considering the L2TL system? How would it be different?
3. Has your view of player-learner agency changed since you read Chapter 2? If so, in what ways? If not, why not? Do you view this as a critical element of our understanding of digital game-mediated L2TL?
4. How do your current teaching activities reflect a learning-to-play perspective? A playing-to-learn perspective? How might you incorporate these views into both game-enhanced and game-based activities in your future L2 contexts?

7.3 THE FUTURE OF DIGITAL GAME-MEDIATED L2TL

The future of game-mediated L2TL is uncertain, exciting, and full of promise, just like the endgame stage of chess or the final battle at the end of a dungeon in a game such as *World of Warcraft*. As we have seen throughout this book, L2TL may be informed, enhanced, and transformed by digital games. Game-mediated L2TL warrants serious attention from, and collaboration among, researchers, practitioners, administrators, and game designers. Looking toward the future of game-mediated L2TL, we conclude with eight insights:

1. *More research.* A key component to successful implementation and evaluation of game-mediated L2TL is going to be the systematic analysis of both game-enhanced and gamed-based implementations. Although the theoretical and practical parallels between games and L2TL are unmistakable, a critical mass of data, from a variety of theoretical perspectives, is needed to substantiate, revise, and advance work in this area. A range of data collection and analysis methods will be both useful and necessary in this endeavor. This includes, but is not limited to, psychometric instruments, pre-post measures of learning outcomes, systematic observation and analysis of real-time gameplay, and perceptive measures such as interviews, focus groups, and surveys. Ideally, each can be used to build a comprehensive body of data informing future design and implementation of digital games in L2TL. We view empirical research as a critical next step and encourage researchers and practitioners alike to engage in research from multiple perspectives, at varied proficiency levels, and in different educational contexts.

2. *Focused research.* As research advances in this area, a primary focus should be a better understanding of what elements are especially effective for specific aspects of L2TL. Although some research has begun in each of the areas discussed here, a great deal of work needs to be done before arriving at a systematic understanding of each. With regard to goals and feedback, this may include, for example, the effects on learning of choice provision, different task and feedback types, and varied task sequences in quests. With regard to motivation, this may include evaluating the implementation of game-mediated applications (both game-enhanced and game-based) or game-informed principles (e.g., game-informed feedback and assessment systems). Research on game-mediated interaction might include studies investigating with-game, through-game, and about-game discourses, and studies on context might look at the interactions of personal and designed narratives, aligning game narratives with curricular topics, or developing critical game literacies.

3. *Collaborations.* We cannot stress enough the importance of collaboration and exchange in further developing a more comprehensive understanding of game-mediated L2TL. Sustained interaction between researchers and practitioners is key to promoting innovative educational practice. This includes, at a minimum, research partnerships (e.g., grant projects, curriculum building, and professional development workshops), student involvement (e.g., the partnership of graduate students, undergraduate students, and/or high school students for the creation and implementation of a digital game), interdisciplinary work between game designers and L2TL practitioners and researchers, cross-institutional work, and shared data sets. Through productive collaboration, a critical mass of information can inform best practices and allow for an understanding that is current with the rapidly evolving technological and social innovations related to digital games. Although we fully recognize the difficulties in sustaining these partnerships (e.g., time constraints, financial limitations), energy well placed has the potential to save a great deal of time and effort in the long run. Possibilities for continued collaboration can be facilitated through national working groups, online communities, and support of interdisciplinary scholarship and teaching.

4. *Renewed perspective.* We believe digital games are, and will become, a prominent piece of many language learners' everyday lives, as they are already a notable part of everyday life in today's society. Concomitant with this shift, game-mediated L2TL should be responsive and thoughtful, that is, proactive rather than reactive. Ultimately, our hope is that educators take advantage of the potential that digital games offer for transformed educational practice, instead of isolating and stigmatizing them as time wasters and addictive vices. We see the thoughtful and systematic integration of games in future L2TL curricula, as opposed to their use as only ancillary, just-for-fun, extracurricular activities. For example, this might include the use of game-enhanced activities related to the *SIMS* in a first-year language course to highlight critical lexical elements such as clothes,

emotions, and daily activities. It might mean the integration of games built specifically for L2TL such as *Zon* or *Mentira* or the use of MMOGs such as *World of Warcraft* or *Diablo III* for the development of new media literacies and involvement in attendant discourses. We see perspectives being renewed already and are hopeful that the ideas in this book continue to challenge and inform L2TL research and practice.

5. ***Measured expectations.*** At the same time, some difficulties and misunderstandings will undoubtedly arise about digital game-mediated L2TL, as is the case with many new endeavors. These challenges can be technical (e.g., limited access to digital games, server errors, or missing devices), time related (e.g., planning and design of new curriculum, assessment rubrics, or lack of in-class time), and attitudinal (e.g., views about digital games as unnecessary, a waste of time, or boring). We hope that this will not discourage work in this area, but rather encourage people to continue working to better understand the best uses of digital games for L2 development. It is also essential to remember that games will not, and should not, do everything, and that they should not be treated as the latest bandwagon.

6. ***Increased diversity.*** We believe that game types and genres will continue to diversify, and that new learning applications will be found for new games, both as integrative, complete learning environments and as smaller games targeted at specific areas. For example, one area in which we see games having an especially strong potential is languages for specific purposes, such as medicine, business, travel, and education. We see the recognition of vernacular games as cultural texts, as useful for L2 learning as a film, novel, or any authentic literacy practice, and the integration of game-enhanced activities into L2TL practice. We also see an increased variety and availability of game-based L2TL environments designed specifically for L2TL purposes. With this diversity, we imagine there will be a variety of quality, with both well-designed and poorly designed games available. We hope that instructors, administrators, learners, and researchers will be able to become critical consumers of these games and not assume that all games are equal. This book, we hope, will be the first of many that offer tools for critical review and awareness.

7. ***Open minds.*** As more and more research is done in the area of game-mediated L2TL, we are beginning to build a body of knowledge to inform decisions about future research and classroom practice. However, because what we know is still relatively limited, we have no doubt that in the future, we will come across factors we have yet to even know we need to know. Furthermore, as technologies evolve, much of what we think we know now will also need to change. We encourage designers, practitioners, administrators, and researchers to keep an eye out and an open mind for innovations and potential game changers. We also encourage those who work in this area to share their successes as well as failures to ensure all can gain from a comprehensive view of the issues at hand.

8. ***Critical play.*** We have no doubt that game types, aesthetics, hardware, and player populations will change and evolve and become more diverse and prominent in everyday society. As these rapid shifts occur, however, it is critical for us to continue playing and interacting with this variety of games and populations so that we can imagine, and ultimately realize, their L2TL potential. Trying to understand and apply games without playing them is like trying to teach with films or novels without watching or reading them. We encourage you to play games in a language you are learning or teaching, keeping the concepts presented in this book in mind. In other words, we invite you to experience firsthand how digital games put language at play. We recommend playing until you are fully engaged, your actions and awareness are one, and you lose track of time—in other words, "go with the flow."

7.4 GAME-MEDIATED APPLICATIONS

In this section, we offer summary tasks that bring together the activities from each of the chapters in the book. They are designed as summary units for both game-enhanced and game-based L2TL in which learners collect and present their knowledge to reflect upon and extend what they have learned. These summary activities require the completion of the majority of the other tasks throughout the book prior to beginning those presented here.

7.4.1 Game-enhanced summary activities

The objective of each of these activities is for L2 learner-players to reflect upon the other game-enhanced activities they have done to reinforce a more comprehensive understanding of games and their role in the L2 learning experience. We present two possible activities—a reflective portfolio and a game plan for L2 learning. You may choose to use one or both of these activities with your students.

Activity 7A: Procedures
1. Prepare, modify, and translate activity instructions as necessary.
2. Have students compile and bring to class all of their previous work on game-enhanced L2TL.
3. In class, present the instructions and objectives of the activity and give examples of the portfolio as needed.
4. Based on the learning context, assign completion of the portfolio. The amount of time spent on the portfolio in and out of class will vary based on each individual context.
5. Have students bring completed portfolios to present to their classmates. Have students talk with three to four peers to present their portfolios.

Note
- The specific requirements for the portfolio will depend on the actual game-enhanced activities done in class. Everything is included here for convenience sake.

ACTIVITY 7A

A reflective portfolio

Create a portfolio in which you compile all of the work you have done examining different parts of games as related to your experience learning [target language]. Based on your previous work, include a 1–2 page reflection in which you think about which games and which parts of games might or might not be helpful for learning [target language]. Your portfolio should include the following:

- 1–2 page reflection
- 2A—Learning the Tutorial
- 2B—Written Game Journal
- 3A—Interacting with Games
- 3B—Interacting Through or Around Games
- 3C—Interacting About Games
- 4A—In-game Feedback
- 4B—Feedback in Attendant Discourses
- 5A—Designing Narratives: Character Descriptions
- 5B—Designing Narratives: Setting Descriptions
- 5C—Designing Narratives: Plot Descriptions
- 6A—Thinking about Flow in Games and Learning
- 6B—Thinking About Engagement in Games and Learning

Activity 7B: Procedures

1. Have students review previous game-enhanced activities and bring them to class.
2. In class, review the main principles of each of the previously completed activities and review Appendix III: Evaluating Digital Games for L2TL. Provide the evaluation guide to all students.
3. Have students work in groups to complete the activity. This can be done during class or as homework.

ACTIVITY 7B

A "game" plan

You have been asked to help select three games to be used in [target class] next year. Utilize what you know about different components of games to select the three that you think would be most effective.

1. Complete the *Evaluating Digital Games for L2TL* evaluation sheet for each game using information from your previous work and new exploration of the game.
2. Write a one-page justification about why you selected the three games for this class. Be sure to use specific examples in your justification.

7.4.2 A game-based L2TL environment: Presenting your design

This activity focuses on bringing together each of the design elements completed as part of other chapters of this book. It asks learners to compile what they have worked on and create a game proposal to present to the grant committee for selection. Depending on the level of the learner, all or part of the activity can be done in the target language. Alternatively, specific components can be designated "target language only."

Procedures

1. Prepare, modify, and translate the activity prompts as necessary.
2. Have students compile previous game-based work and bring it to class to share with their peers. Explain the objective to the students.
3. In class, have students divide into groups of three to four and present their design work to one another. Based on this in-class discussion, have each group select one general game design idea to fully develop into a presentation and proposal.
4. Have students work in groups to prepare an oral presentation and written proposal for the game design company. This will take approximately one to two weeks.
5. Organize an in-class session during which students present their ideas based on the given parameters and have two to three game company representatives (e.g., other teachers, parent volunteers, teaching assistants, peers) select the best proposal and presentation.

ACTIVITY 7C

Game design proposal

A game design company has requested proposals for the development of a game in [target language]. You already have a good start from the other design work you have been doing and decide to apply for the grant money. You may use this work in your final proposal. As a group, prepare the following items to present to the representatives of the game design company on [insert date]. The representatives will judge each of the proposals and select their favorite. Be sure to include as much detailed information as possible. Your grant proposal should include an oral presentation and written proposal in which you include the following:

1. Basic Information
   a. Intended Learning Objectives
   b. Genre of the Game
   c. Object of the Game
   d. Context of the Game (setting, characters, etc.)
2. Tasks
   a. Summary of Task Types
   b. Sample Task (in the target language)
      i. Objective
      ii. Rewards

      iii. Procedure
      iv. Dialogue

3. Interaction
   a. Summary of Interaction Types
   b. Sample Interactions
      i. Formal Interaction
      ii. Social Interaction
      iii. Cultural Interaction
      iv. Sample Dialogue

4. Feedback
   a. Summary of Feedback Types
   b. Sample Feedback Mechanism (two examples)
      i. Player Presentation
      ii. Language
      iii. Objective

5. Context
   a. Summary of Context
   b. Narrative Description (including the setting, characters, and story)

6. Motivation
   a. Summary of Motivation Elements
   b. Sample Motivating Elements (two examples)
      i. Player Presentation
      ii. Language
      iii. Objective

You may include as many images and examples in your proposal as you wish. Be creative and have fun!

7.5 SUGGESTED READINGS

This section provides a starting place for those interested in continued work in this area. It includes twelve book-length treatments of the key concepts discussed in each of the chapters of this book. The first six are specifically related to L2TL and the second six to game design. They inform many of the fundamental ideas presented in this book. These should be viewed as a starting point, rather than a comprehensive list and can be used in conjunction with many of the journal articles and other books referenced throughout this volume.

7.5.1 L2TL

Cook, G. (2000). *Language Play, Language Learning*. Oxford, UK: Oxford University Press.
In this thought-provoking book, applied linguist Guy Cook explores the phenomenon of language play, which involves the patterning of linguistic form, the creation of alternative realities, and the social use of both of these for intimacy

and conflict (p. 5). He examines the forms, meanings, and uses of language play and presents theories on why it occurs and its role in human development, specifically in language learning. He also considers implications for language teaching, and how current communicative approaches do not always account for language play, because of their apparent focus on meaning. Cook's book is fundamental for understanding the intimate relationships between playing with language and learning it.

Dörnyei, Z., and Ushioda, E., Eds. (2009). *Motivation, Identity and the L2 Self.* **Bristol, UK, and Buffalo, NY: Multilingual Matters.**
In this book, Zoltan Dörnyei and Ema Ushioda summarize the L2 ideal self model of motivation. This is followed by a compilation of various studies by a variety of authors who have utilized this model in L2 research. This includes an examination of the model itself as well as empirical research on the application of the model.

Halliday, M., and Webster, J. (2009). *The Essential Halliday.* **London: Continuum.**
Because systemic-functional linguistics (SFL) is an extensive field, it can sometimes be difficult to find a starting point. Whereas there are other primers, this recent volume provides a cultivated selection of fundamental writings by the father of SFL, Michael Halliday. The volume presents essential writings on function, grammar, learning and teaching, and discourse analysis, among other areas. Readers of this work will gain a substantial grounding for further research in SFL.

Kern, R. (2000). *Literacy and Language Teaching.* **New York: Oxford University Press.**
Richard Kern presents a sociocultural perspective on literacy practice and offers an L2 pedagogical framework based on the idea of available designs. The framework is applied to all aspects of literacy (reading and writing) instruction, including grammar, vocabulary, cohesion/coherence, and style. Although Kern does not discuss digital gaming specifically, his framework can be adapted if games are understood as sociocultural texts and practices, so that the linguistic and schematic elements in games can serve as resources for L2 learning.

Lantolf, J., and Thorne, S. (2006). *Sociocultural Theory and the Genesis of Second Language Development.* **Oxford, UK: Oxford University Press.**
In this work, James Lantolf and Steven Thorne make an intensive and comprehensive application of and cultural-historical activity theory to L2 learning and teaching, and they address theory, research, and practice. They discuss key concepts such as mediation, internalization, activity, and the ZPD, exploring their histories and considering how sociocultural theory pioneers such as Vygotsky, who never wrote specifically about L2TL, would apply them to the field.

Van den Branden, K., Bygate, M., and Norris, J. (2009). *Task-Based Language Teaching: A Reader.* **Amsterdam: John Benjamins.**
Edited by three leading experts in the field, this volume provides an introduction to the history and theoretical background of task-based language teaching (TBLT). This is followed by a compilation of previously published seminal work

in TBLT. The reader is divided into four areas—introduction to TBLT; curriculum, syllabus, and task design; variables affecting TBLT; and assessment—with each focusing on fundamental considerations in TBLT. This volume is especially useful for those just beginning work in this area or wishing to reinforce baseline knowledge related to TBLT.

7.5.2 Digital gaming

Czikszentmihalyi, M. (2008). *Flow: The Psychology of Optimal Experience.* **New York: Harper.**
Mihaly Czikszentmihalyi presents a research-based, user-friendly summary of the psychological concepts associated with his notion of *flow* and its relationship to happiness. The book is intended for the non-expert reader, but also contains extensive resources for those who wish to pursue a more scholarly approach to any of the topics of the book. It includes 10 chapters that address issues such as the conditions of the flow experience and finding happiness in numerous situations. This book will be especially interesting for those wanting to further consider flow as a fundamental concept in good digital games.

Fullerton, T. (2008). *Game Design Workshop: A Playcentric Approach to Creating Innovative Games* **(2nd ed). Burlington, MA: Elsevier.**
In this approachable and hands-on book, Tracy Fullerton provides a balance of theory and practical guidance in how to design digital games. Using real-world examples and incorporating viewpoints from field leaders, she leads readers through the steps of game development, including prototyping, play testing, and documenting.

Gee, J. (2007). *What Video Games Have to Teach Us About Learning and Literacy* **(2nd ed.) New York: Palgrave Macmillan.**
In this second edition of his groundbreaking book, James Gee explores many fundamental concepts related to digital games and learning, such as the role of situated meaning, identity, cultural models, and agency. He includes an explanation of 36 learning principles stemming from digital games, many of which correspond with notions we discuss in this book, including goal orienting, interaction, and feedback as instruction. He ultimately argues that digital gaming can develop the literacies necessary for the future.

Juul, J. (2005). *Half-Real: Video Games Between Rules and Fictional Worlds.* **Cambridge, MA: MIT Press.**
Jesper Juul presents a compelling discussion of video games, and how they challenge traditional definitions of games as simply rule-based systems of interaction, by virtue of the fictional worlds in which they are embedded. He argues that in games, "rules and fiction interact, compete, and complement each other" (p. 163), and that games are "playgrounds where players can experiment with doing things they would or would not normally do" (p. 193). His book provides a thorough and interesting discussion of the complex theories, history, and designs behind video games.

Salen, K., and Zimmerman, E. (2005). *Rules of Play: Game Design Fundamentals.* **Cambridge, MA: The MIT Press.**

Katie Salen and Eric Zimmerman offer a comprehensive tome that covers every aspect of game design theory and practice. Throughout the book, they describe the various components of task creation and provide examples of the types of designs that create meaningful gameplay and, as a result, a successful game. Organized under three primary schemas of rules, play, and culture, concepts such as choice and interactivity are discussed as fundamental components of digital games. These fundamentals "include the powerful connection between the rules of a game and the play that the rules engender, the pleasures games invoke, the meanings they construct, the ideologies they embody, and the stories they tell" (p. 6).

Schell, J. (2008). *The Art of Game Design.* **Burlington, MA: Morgan Kauffman Publishers.**

In this game design book, Jesse Schell provides a unique perspective on game design that compliments much of the other work in the field. It is easily accessible, complex, and user friendly. Through the reflection on game design from a variety of perspectives, framed as 100 lenses, Schell challenges the designer to consider the balance of numerous factors when making game design decisions. The book includes 33 chapters that lead the reader through examining his or her role as designer, the fundamentals of game design, and the practicalities associated with game development.

REFERENCES

Aarseth, E. (2003). A hollow world: World of Warcraft as spatial practice. In H. Corneliussen and J. Rettberg, eds., *Digital Culture, Play, and Identity: A World of Warcraft Reader* (pp. 111–122). Cambridge, MA: MIT Press.

Allen, H. W. (2009). A literacy-based approach to the advanced French writing course. *The French Review, 83,* 368–385.

Allen, H. W., and Paesani, K. (2010). Exploring the feasibility of a pedagogy of multiliteracies in introductory foreign language courses. *L2 Journal, 2,* 119–142.

Anderson, R. (1977). The notion of schemata and the educational enterprise: General discussion of the conference. In R. C. Anderson, R. J. Spiro, and W. E. Montague, eds., *Schooling and the Acquisition of Knowledge* (pp. 415-431). Hillsdale, NJ: Lawrence Erlbaum Associates.

Arnseth, H. C. (2006). Learning to play or playing to learn—A critical account of the models of communication informing educational research on computer gameplay. *Game Studies, 6*(1). Available online at http://gamestudies.org/0601/articles/arnseth

Atkinson, D. (2002). Toward a sociocognitive approach to second language acquisition. *Modern Language Journal, 86*(4), 525–545.

Bardovi-Harlig, K. (2001). Evaluating the empirical evidence: Grounds for instruction in pragmatics? In K. Rose and G. Kasper, eds., *Pragmatics in Language Teaching* (pp. 13–32). Cambridge, UK: Cambridge University Press.

Bell, N. (2005). Exploring L2 language play as an aid to SLL: A case study of humour in NS-NNS interaction. *Applied Linguistics, 26*(2), 192–218.

Belz, J. (2002). Second language play as a representation of the multicompetent self in foreign language study. *Journal of Language, Identity, and Education, 1,* 13–39.

Belz, J., and Reinhardt, J. (2004). Aspects of advanced foreign language proficiency: Internet-mediated German language play. *International Journal of Applied Linguistics, 14*(3), 324–362.

Block, D. (2003). *The Social Turn in Second Language Acquisition.* Washington, DC: Georgetown University Press.

Breen, M. (1987). Learner contributions to task design. In C. Candlin and D. Murphy, eds., *Language Learning Tasks* (pp. 23-46). Englewood Cliffs, NJ: Prentice Hall.

Breen, M. (1997). Information does not equal knowledge: Theorizing the political economy of virtuality. *Journal of Computer-Mediated Communication, 3,* 0. doi: 10.1111/j.1083-6101.1997.tb00076.x

Breen, M. P., and Candlin, C. (1980). The essentials of a communicative curriculum in language teaching. *Applied Linguistics, 1*(2), 89–112.

Browell, D. E. (2007). World of studentcraft: An ethnographic study on the engagement of traditional students within an online world. Capella University. Available at http://ezproxy.library.arizona.edu/login?url=http://search.proquest.com/docview/304699137?accountid=8360

Brown, D. (2007). *Principles of Language Learning and Teaching* (5th ed.). New York: Pearson Longman.

Bryant, T. (2006). Using World of Warcraft and other MMORPGs to foster a targeted, social, and cooperative approach toward language learning. *Academic Commons, The Library*. Available at http://www.academiccommons.org/commons/essay/bryant-MMORPGs-for-SLA

Caillois, R. (1961). *Man, Play, and Games*. Glencoe, IL: The Free Press.

Calleja, G. (2007). Digital game involvement: A conceptual model. *Games and Culture, 2*(3), 236–260.

Carr, D. (2006). Games and narrative. In D. Carr, D. Buckingham, A. Burn, and A. Schott, eds., *Computer Games: Text, Narrative, and Play* (pp. 30–44). Cambridge, UK: Polity.

Cohen, A. D. (1997). Developing pragmatic ability: Insights from the accelerated study of Japanese. *New Trends and Issues in Teaching Japanese Language and Culture, 3*(15), 133–150.

Cohen, A. D. (2011). *Strategies in Learning and Using a Second Language* (2nd ed.). Harlow, UK: Longman/Pearson Education.

Cook, G. (2000). *Language Play, Language Learning*. Oxford, UK: Oxford University Press.

Cornillie, F., Desmet, P., and Clarebout, G. (2012). Between learning and playing? Exploring learners' perceptions of corrective feedback in an immersive game for English pragmatics. *ReCALL, 24*(3), 257–278.

Coughlan, P., and Duff, P. (1994). Same task, different activities: Analysis of a SLA task from an activity theory perspective. In J. Lantolf and G. Appel, eds., *Vygotskian Approaches to Second Language Research* (pp. 173–194). Norwood, NJ: Ablex.

Crystal, D. (2001). *Language Play*. Chicago: University of Chicago Press.

Czikszentmihalyi, M. (1990, 2008). *Flow: The Psychology of Optimal Experience*. New York: Harper.

de Bot, B. K. (1996). The psycholinguistics of the output hypothesis. *Language Learning, 46*(3), 529–555.

deHaan, J., Reed, W. M., and Kuwada, K. (2010). The effect of interactivity with a music video game on second language vocabulary recall. *Language Learning and Technology, 14*(2), 74–94.

Dörnyei, Z. (2001). *Teaching and Researching Motivation*. Harlow, UK/New York: Longman.

Dörnyei, Z. (2005). *The Psychology of the Language Learner: Individual Differences in Second Language Acquisition*. London: Lawrence Erlbaum Associates.

Dörnyei, Z. (2009). *The Psychology of Second Language Acquisition*. Oxford, UK: Oxford University Press.

Doughty, C., and Williams, J. (1998). *Focus on Form in Classroom Second Language Acquisition*. Cambridge, UK: Cambridge University Press.

Duff, P. (2008). Language socialization, participation and identity: Ethnographic approaches. In M. Martin-Jones, A.-M. de Mejia, and N. Hornberger, eds., *Encyclopedia of Language and Education: Vol. 3. Discourse and Education* (pp. 107–119). New York: Springer Verlag.

Duff, P. (2012). Second language socialization. In A. Duranti, E. Ochs, and B. Schieffelin, eds., *Handbook of Language Socialization* (pp. 564–586). New York: Blackwell.

Dunn, W. E., and Lantolf, J. P. (1998). Vygotsky's zone of proximal development and Krashen's i + 1: Incommensurable constructs; incommensurable theories. *Language Learning, 48*(3), 411–442.

Ellis, R. (2003). *Task-Based Language Learning and Teaching*. Oxford, UK: Oxford University Press.

Fauconnier, G., and Turner, M. (2002). *The Way We Think: Conceptual Blending and the Mind's Hidden Complexities*. New York: Basic Books.

Felicia, P. (2011). *Handbook of Research on Improving Learning and Motivation Through Educational Games: Multidisciplinary Approaches*. Hershey, PA: Information Science Reference.

Filsecker, M., and Bündgens, J. (2012). Behaviorism, constructivism, and communities of practice: How pedagogic theories help us understand game-based language learning. In H. Reinders, ed., *Digital Games in Language Learning and Teaching* (pp. 50-69). New York: Palgrave Macmillan.

Firth, A., and Wagner, J. (1997). On discourse, communication, and (some) fundamental concepts in SLA research. *Modern Language Journal, 81*, 285–300.

Frasca, G. (1999). Ludology meets narratology: Similitude and differences between video (games) and narrative. Parnasso #3. Helsinki. Available at http://www.ludology.org/articles/ludology.htm

Fullerton, T. (2008). *Game Design Workshop: A Playcentric Approach to Creating Innovative Games*. Amsterdam: Elsevier.

Gardner, R. C., and Lambert, W. (1972). *Attitudes and Motivation in Second Language Learning*. Rowley, MA: Newbury House.

Gardner, R. C., and MacIntyre, P. D. (1991). An instrumental motivation in language study: Who says it isn't effective? *Studies in Second Language Acquisition, 13*(1), 57–72.

Gass, S. M. (1997). *Input, Interaction, and the Second Language Learner*. Mahwah, NJ: Lawrence Erlbaum Associates.

Gass, S. M., and Selinker, L. (2001). *Second Language Acquisition: An Introductory Course*. London: Lawrence Erlbaum Associates.

Gee, J. P. (2003). *What Video Games Have to Teach Us About Learning and Literacy*. New York: Palgrave Macmillan.

Gee, J. P. (2004). *Situated Language and Learning: A Critique of Traditional Schooling*. London: Routledge.

Gee, J. P. (2005). *Why Video Games Are Good for Your Soul: Pleasure and Learning*. Melbourne, Vic.: Common Ground Publishing.

Gee, J. P. (2007). *What Video Games Have to Teach Us About Learning and Literacy* (2nd ed.). New York: Palgrave Macmillan.

Hager, M. (2004). Using geography and a story-based approach in the beginning German classroom. *Die Unterrichtspraxis/Teaching German, 37*(2), 165–169.

Halliday, M. A. K. (1978). *Language as Social Semiotic: The Social Interpretation of Language and Meaning*. London: Edward Arnold.

Halliday, M. A. K., and Hasan, R. (1989). *Language, Context, and Text: Aspects of Language in a Social-semiotic Perspective*. Oxford: Oxford University Press.

Holden, C., and Sykes, J. (2011). Leveraging mobile games for place-based language learning. *International Journal of Game-based Learning, 1*(2), 1–18.

Huizinga, J. (1938). *Homo ludens*. London: Routledge.

Hymes, D. (1972). On communicative competence. In J. Pride and J. Holmes, eds., *Sociolinguistics* (pp. 269–293). Harmondsworth, Middlesex, UK: Penguin Education.

Ishihara, N., and Tarone, E. (2009). Emulating and resisting pragmatic norms: Learner subjectivity and foreign language pragmatic use. In N. Noguchi, ed., *Pragmatic Competence in Japanese as a Second Language* (pp. 101–128). Berlin, Germany: Mouton Pragmatics Series: Mouton de Gruyter.

Juul, J. (2005). *Half-Real: Video Games Between Real Rules and Fictional Worlds*. Cambridge, MA: MIT Press.

Kern, R. (2000). *Literacy and Language Teaching*. Oxford, UK: Oxford University Press.

Krashen, S. D. (1984). *Principles and Practice in Second Language Acquisition*. Oxford, UK: Pergamon Press.

Kumaravadivelu, B. (1991). Language learning tasks: Teacher intention and learner interpretation. *ELT Journal, 45*, 98–107.

Kumaravadivelu, B. (2006). *Understanding Language Teaching: From Method to Postmethod*. Mahwah, NJ: Lawrence Erlbaum Associates.

Lacasa, P., Martínez, R., and Méndez, L. (2008). Developing new literacies using commercial videogames as educational tools. *Linguistics and Education, 19*, 85–106.

Lakoff, G., and Johnson, M. (1980). *Metaphors We Live By*. Chicago: University of Chicago Press.

Lam, W. S. E. (2000). Second language literacy and the design of the self: A case study of a teenager writing on the Internet. *TESOL Quarterly, 34*, 457–483.

Lamb, M. (2004). Integrative motivation in a globalizing world. *System: An International Journal of Educational Technology and Applied Linguistics, 32*(1), 3–19.

Lankshear, C., and Knobel, M. (2006). *New Literacies: Changing Knowledge and Classroom Learning* (2nd ed.). Philadelphia: Open University Press.

Lantolf, J. P. (1997). Language play and the acquisition of L2 Spanish. In W. Glass and A. T. Perez-Leroux, eds., *Contemporary Perspectives on the Acquisition of Spanish. Volume 2: Production, Processing and Comprehension* (pp. 3–24). Somerville, MA: Cascadilla Press.

Lantolf, J. P. (2000). *Sociocultural Theory and Second Language Learning*. Oxford, UK: Oxford University Press.

Lantolf, J. P., and Appel, G. (1994). Theoretical framework: An introduction to Vygotskian perspectives on second language research. In J. Lantolf and G. Appel, eds., *Vygotskian Approaches to Second Language Research* (pp. 1–32). Norwood, NJ: Ablex.

Lantolf, J. P., and Thorne, S. L. (2006). *Sociocultural Theory and the Genesis of Second Language Development*. Oxford, UK: Oxford University Press.

Larsen-Freeman, D., and Anderson, M. (2011). *Techniques and Principles in Language Teaching*. Oxford, UK: Oxford University Press.

Larsen-Freeman, D., and Cameron, R. (2008). *Complex Systems and Applied Linguistics*. Oxford, UK: Oxford University Press.

Lave, J., and Wenger, E. (1991). *Situated Learning: Legitimate Peripheral Participation*. Cambridge, UK: Cambridge University Press.

Lee, J., and Hoadley, C. (2007). Leveraging identity to make learning fun: Possible selves and experiential learning in massively multiplayer online games (MMOGs). *Innovate, 3*(6). Available at http://www.innovateonline.info/pdf/vol3_issue6/leveraging_identity_to_make_learning_fun-__possible_selves_and_experiential_learning_in_massively_multiplayer_online_games_(mmogs).pdf

Leontiev, A. (1978). *Activity, Consciousness and Personality*. Englewood Cliffs, NJ: Prentice Hall.

LoCastro, V. (2003). *An Introduction to Pragmatics: Social Action for Language Teachers*. Ann Arbor: University of Michigan Press.

Long, M. H. (1983). Linguistic and conversational adjustments to non-native speakers. *Studies in Second Language Acquisition, 25*, 37–63.

Long, M. H. (1996). The role of the linguistic environment in second language acquisition. In W. C. Ritchie and T. K. Bahtia, eds., *Handbook of Second Language Acquisition* (pp. 413–468). New York: Academic Press.

Long, M. H., and Robinson, P. (1998). Focus on form: Theory, research and practice. In C. Doughty and J. Williams, eds., *Focus on Form in Second Language Acquisition* (pp. 15–41). Cambridge, UK: Cambridge University Press.

Malinowski, B. (1923). The problem of meaning in primitive languages. In C. K. Ogden and I. A. Richards, eds., *The Meaning of Meaning* (pp. 146–152). London: Routledge and Kegan Paul.

McLaughlin, B. (1987). *Theories of Second Language Learning*. London: Hodder.

Miller, M., and Hegelheimer, V. (2006). The SIMS meet ESL: Incorporating authentic computer simulation games into the language classroom. *Interactive Technology and Smart Education, 4*, 311–328.

Mishan, F. (2004). *Designing Authenticity into Language Learning Materials.* Bristol, UK: Intellect, Ltd.

Nardi, B., Ly, S., and Harris, J. (2007). Learning conversations in World of Warcraft. *The Proceedings of the 2007 Hawaii International Conference on Systems Science.* New York: IEEE Press.

Nassaji, H., and Cumming, A. (2000). What's a ZPD? A case study of a young ESL student and teacher interacting through dialogue journals. *Language Teaching Research, 4*(2), 95–121.

Neitzel, B. (2005). Narrativity in computer games. In J. Raessens and J. Goldstein, eds., *Handbook of Computer Game Studies* (pp. 227–249). Cambridge, MA: MIT Press.

Neville, D. (2010). Structuring narrative in 3D digital game-based learning environments to support second language acquisition. *Foreign Language Annals, 43*(3), 446–469.

New London Group. (1996). A pedagogy of multiliteracies. *Harvard Educational Review, 66*(1), 60–92.

Nunan, D. (1989). *Designing Tasks for the Communicative Classroom.* Cambridge, UK: Cambridge University Press.

Nunan, D. (2004). *Task-Based Language Teaching.* Cambridge, UK: Cambridge University Press.

Ochs, E., and Schieffelin, D. (1984). Language acquisition and socialization: Three developmental stories. In R. Shweder and R. LeVine, eds., *Culture Theory: Mind, Self, and Emotion* (pp. 276–322). Cambridge, UK: Cambridge University Press.

Omaggio Hadley, A. (2001). *Teaching Language in Context.* Boston: Heinle and Heinle.

Oxford, R. (2006) Task-based language teaching and learning: An overview. *Asian EFL Journal, 8*(3). Available at http://www.asian-efl-journal.com/Sept_06_ro.php

Pellettieri, J. (2000). Negotiation in cyberspace: The role of chatting in the development of communicative competence. In M. Warschauer and R. Kern, eds., *Network-Based Language Teaching: Concepts and Practice* (pp. 59–86). Cambridge, UK: Cambridge University Press.

Pica, T., Kanagy, R., and Falodun, J. (1993). Choosing and using communicative tasks for second language instruction. In G. Crookes and S. Gass, eds., *Tasks and Language Learning: Integrating Theory and Practice.* Clevedon, UK/Philadelphia: Multilingual Matters.

Piiranen-Marsh, A., and Tainio, L. (2009). Other-repetition as a resource for participation in the activity of playing a video game. *Modern Language Journal, 93*(2), 153–169.

Pomerantz, A., and Bell, N. (2007). Learning to play, playing to learn: FL learners as multicompetent language users. *Applied Linguistics, 28*(4), 556–578.

Prabhu, N. (1987). *Second Language Pedagogy.* Oxford, UK: Oxford University Press.

Prensky, M. (2001). *Digital Game-Based Learning.* New York: McGraw-Hill.

Prensky, M. (2006). *"Don't Bother Me Mom, I'm Learning!": How Computer and Video Games Are Preparing Your Kids for Twenty-First Century Success and How You Can Help!* St. Paul, MN: Paragon House.

Purushotma, R. (2005). You're not studying, you're just … *Language Learning and Technology, 9*(1), 80–96.

Purushotma, R., Thorne, S. L., and Wheatley, J. (2008). Language learning and video games. Paper produced for the Open Language and Learning Games Project, Massachusetts Institute of Technology, funded by the William and Flora Hewlett Foundation. Available at http://knol.google.com/k/ravi-purushotma/10-key-principles-for-designing-video/27mkxqba7b13/2

Reinders, H., and Wattana, S. (2012). Talk to me! Games and students' willingness to communicate. In H. Reinders, ed., *Digital Games in Language Learning and Teaching* (pp. 156-187). New York: Palgrave Macmillan

Reinhardt, J. (2008). Negotiating meaningfulness: An enhanced perspective on interaction in computer-mediated foreign language learning environments. In S. Magnan, ed., *Mediated Discourse Online* (pp. 219–244). Amsterdam: John Benjamins.

Reinhardt, J. (2012). Accommodating divergent frameworks in analysis of technology-mediated interaction. In M. Dooly and R. O'Dowd, eds., *Researching Online Interaction and Exchange in Foreign Language Education: Current Trends and Issues* (pp. 45-77). Frankfurt: Peter Lang.

Reinhardt, J., and Sykes, J. (2011). Framework for game-enhanced materials development. CERCLL G2T Project White Paper Series. Tucson, AZ: Center for Educational Resources in Culture, Language and Literacy.

Reinhardt, J., and Sykes, J. (2012). Conceptualizing digital game-mediated L2 learning and pedagogy: Game-enhanced and game-based research and practice. In H. Reinders, ed., *Digital Games in Language Learning and Teaching* (pp. 32-49). New York: Palgrave Macmillan.

Reinhardt, J., and Thorne, S. L. (2011). Beyond comparisons: Frameworks for developing digital L2 literacies. In N. Arnold and L. Ducate, eds., *Present and Future Promises of CALL: From Theory and Research to New Directions in Language Teaching* (pp. 257–280). San Marcos, TX: CALICO.

Reinhardt, J., and Zander, V. (2011). Social networking in an intensive English program classroom: A language socialization perspective. *CALICO Journal, 28*(2), 326–344.

Richards, J. C., and Rodgers, T. S. (2001). *Approaches and Methods in Language Teaching* (2nd ed.). Cambridge, UK: Cambridge University Press.

Russell, J., and Spada, N. (2006). The effectiveness of corrective feedback for the acquisition of L2 grammar: A meta-analysis of the research. In J. Norris and L. Ortega, eds., *Synthesizing Research in Language Learning and Teaching* (pp. 133–164). Amsterdam: John Benjamins.

Salen, K., and Zimmerman, E. (2004). *Rules of Play: Game Design Fundamentals*. Cambridge, MA: MIT Press.

Samuda, V., and Bygate, M. (2008). *Tasks in Second Language Learning*. Basingstoke, UK: Palgrave Macmillan.

Savignon, S. J. (1972). *Communicative Competence: An Experiment in Foreign Language Teaching*. Philadelphia: Center for Curriculum Development.

Schell, J. (2008). *The Art of Game Design*. Burlington, MA: Morgan Kauffman Publishers.

Schmidt, R. (1990). The role of consciousness in second language learning. *Applied Linguistics, 11,* 129–158.

Sfard, A. (1998). On two metaphors for learning and the dangers of choosing just one. *Educational Researcher, 2*(2), 4–13.

Shrum, J. L., and Glisan, E. W. (2010). *Teacher's Handbook: Contextualized Language Instruction* (4th ed.). Boston: Heinle.

Simons, J. (2007). Narrative, games, and theory. *Game Studies* 7, 1. Available at http://gamestudies.org/0701/articles/simons

Skehan, P. (1998). Task-based instruction. *Annual Review of Applied Linguistics, 18,* 268–286.

Smith, B. (2003). Computer-mediated negotiated interaction: An expanded model. *Modern Language Journal, 87,* 38–57.

Squire, K. D., and Steinkuehler, C. (2006). Generating cyberculture/s: The case of Star Wars Galaxies. In D. Gibbs and K.-L. Krause, eds., *Cyberlines 2.0 Languages and Cultures of the Internet* (pp. 177–198). Albert Park, Australia: James Nicholas Publishers.

Steinkuehler, C. (2007). Massively multiplayer online gaming as a constellation of literacy practices. *eLearning, 4,* 297–318.

Sundqvist, P., and Kerstin Sylvén, L. (2012). World of VoccCraft: Computer games and Swedish learners' L2 English Vocabulary. In H. Reinders, ed., *Digital Games in Language Learning and Teaching* (pp. 189-208). New York: Palgrave Macmillan.

Swain, M. (1995). Three functions of output in second language learning. In G. Cook and G. Seidhofer, eds., *Principles and Practice in Applied Linguistics: Studies in Honor of H. G. Widdowson* (pp. 125–144). Oxford, UK: Oxford University Press.

Swain, M. (2005). The output hypothesis: Theory and research. In E. Hinkel, ed., *Handbook of Research in Second Language* (pp. 471–483). Mahwah, NJ: Lawrence Erlbaum Associates.

Sykes, J. (2008). A dynamic approach to social interaction: Synthetic immersive environments and Spanish pragmatics. Unpublished doctoral dissertation, University of Minnesota, Minneapolis.

Sykes, J. (2009). Learner requests in Spanish: Examining the potential of multiuser virtual environments for L2 pragmatic acquisition. In L. Lomika and G. Lord, eds., *The Second Generation: Online Collaboration and Social Networking in CALL, 2009 CALICO Monograph* (pp. 199–234). San Marcos, TX: CALICO.

Sykes, J. (2010). Multi-user virtual environments: User-driven design and implementation for language learning. In G. Vicenti and J. Braman, eds., *Teaching Through Multi-user Virtual Environments: Applying Dynamic Elements to the Modern Classroom* (pp. 285-305). Hershey, PA: IGI Global.

Sykes, J., and Holden, C. (2011). Communities: Exploring digital games and social networking. In L. Ducate and N. Arnold, eds., *Present and Future Promises of*

CALL: From Theory and Research to New Directions in Language Teaching, CALICO Monograph 2011 (pp. 311–336).

Sykes, J., Oskoz, A., and Thorne, S. L. (2008). Web 2.0, synthetic immersive environments, and the future of language education. *CALICO Journal, 25*(3), 528–546.

Sykes, J., Reinhardt, J., and Thorne, S. L. (2010). Multiplayer digital games as sites for research and practice. In F. Hult, ed., *Directions and Prospects for Educational Linguistics* (pp. 117–136). New York: Springer.

Taylor, T. L. (2006). *Play Between Worlds: Exploring Online Game Culture*. Cambridge, MA: MIT Press.

Thomas, M. (2012). Contextualizing digital game-based language learning: Transformational paradigm shift or business as usual. In H. Reinders, ed., *Digital Games in Language Learning and Teaching* (pp. 11–31). New York: Palgrave Macmillan

Thorne, S. L. (2003). Artifacts and cultures-of-use in intercultural communication. *Language Learning and Technology, 7*(2), 38–67.

Thorne, S. L. (2008). Transcultural communication in open Internet environments and massively multiplayer online games. In S. Magnan, ed., *Mediating Discourse Online* (pp. 305–327). Amsterdam: John Benjamins.

Thorne, S. L. (2012). Gaming writing: Supervernaculars, stylization, and semotic remediation. In G. Kessler, A. Oskoz, and I. Elola, eds., *Technology Across Writing Contexts and Tasks* (pp. 297–316). San Marcos, TX: CALICO Monograph.

Thorne, S. L., and Black, R. W. (2007). New media literacies, online gaming, and language education. CALPER Working Papers Series, No.8. University Park, PA: The Pennsylvania State University, Center for Advanced Language Proficiency Education and Research.

Thorne, S. L., Black, R. W., and Sykes, J. (2009). Second language use, socialization, and learning in Internet communities and online games. *Modern Language Journal, 93*, 802–821.

Thorne, S. L., and Reinhardt, J. (2008). "Bridging activities," new media literacies and advanced foreign language proficiency. *CALICO Journal*, 25(3), 558-572.

Thorne, S. L., Reinhardt, J., and Golombek, P. (2008). Mediation as objectification in the development of professional academic discourse: A corpus-informed curricular innovation. In J. Lantolf and M. Poehner, eds., *Sociocultural Theory and the Teaching of Second Languages* (pp. 256–284). London: Equinox.

Van den Branden, K. (2006). *Task-Based Language Education: From Theory to Practice*. Cambridge, UK: Cambridge University Press.

Van den Branden, K., Bygate, M., and Norris, J. (2009). *Task-Based Language Teaching: A Reader*. Amsterdam: John Benjamins.

van Lier, L. (2004). *The Ecology and Semiotics of Language Learning*. New York: Springer.

Varonis, E., and Gass, S. M. (1985). Non-native/non-native conversations: A model for negotiation of meaning. *Applied Linguistics, 6*, 71–90.

Vygotsky, L. S. (1978). *Mind in Society: The Development of Higher Psychological Processes*. Cambridge, MA: Harvard University Press.

Vygotsky, L. S. (1987). *Thought and Language*. Cambridge, MA: MIT Press.

Warden, C. A., and Lin, H. J. (2000). Existence of integrative motivation in an Asian EFL setting. *Foreign Language Annals, 33*(5), 535–547.

White, L. (1987). Against comprehensible input: The input hypothesis and the development of second-language competence. *Applied Linguistics, 8*(2), 95–110.

Widdowson, H. (1978). *Teaching Language as Communication*. Oxford, UK: Oxford University Press.

Williams, T. A., Bygate, M., and Norris, J. M., eds. (2010). Task-based language teaching: A reader. *ELT Journal, 64*(3), 351–354.

Willis, J. (1996). *A Framework for Tasked-Based Learning*. London: Longman.

Zheng, D., Young, M., Wagner, M., and Brewer, R. (2009). Negotiation for action: English language learning in game-based virtual worlds. *Modern Language Journal, 93*(4), 489–511.

List of Games from Chapters 1–7

Title	Developer	Publisher	Date of First Release
Angry Birds	Rovio Entertainment	Chillingo	2009
Bakery Story	Team Lava	Team Lava	2010
Cityville	Zynga	Zynga	2010
Croquelandia	Sykes, Moore, and Wenland	University of Minnesota	2008
Diablo 3	Blizzard Entertainment	Blizzard Entertainment	2012
Everquest	Sony	Sony	1999
Farm Frenzy 3	Alawar Melesta	Alawar	2011
Final Fantasy X	Square	Square Electronic Arts	2001
Life Quest	Big Fish Games	Big Fish Games	2010
Maggie's Bakery	Little Horse	Maggiemarket	2004
Mario Kart	Nintendo	Nintendo	1992
Mentira	Holden/Sykes	University of New Mexico	2010
Plants vs. Zombies	PopCap Games	Electronic Arts	2009
Poupee Girl	Poupéegirl, inc.	Poupéegirl, inc.	2008
Quest Atlantis	Barab	Indiana University	2008
RU Emergency Response	Sioux Games Production	Youda Games	2008
Runescape	Jagex Games Studio	Jagex Games Studio	2001
Super Mario Brothers	Nintendo Creative Department	Nintendo	1985
The Sims	Maxis	Electronic Arts	2000
Treasures of Mystery Island	Alawar Entertainment	Alawar Entertainment	2012
World of Warcraft	Blizzard Entertainment	Blizzard Entertainment	2004
Youda Sushi Chef	Sioux Games Production	Youda Games	2009
Zon	Zhao et al	Michigan State University	2008

List of Games from Appendix 2: Guide to Game Types and Genres

Title	Developer	Publisher	Date of First Release
Call of Duty	Activision	Activision	2003
Civilization	Meier/Shelley	MicroProse	1991
Diner Dash	GameLab	PlayFirst	2003
Farkle (Zilch)	Sierra Games	Sierra Games	2008
Farmville	Zynga	Zynga	2009

(continued)

Title	Developer	Publisher	Date of First Release
Halo	Bungie, Gearbox, Westlake Interactive	Microsoft Game Studios MacSoft	2001
Heavy Rain	Quantic Dream	Sony Computer Entertainment	2010
Legend of Zelda	Nintendo Capcorn/Flagship Vanpool Grezzo Monolith Soft	Nintendo	1986 (first release)
Myst	Cyan	Brøderbund, Midway Games, Mean Hamster Software, Sunsoft, Maximum Family Games, Funbox Media	1993
PacMan	Namco	Namco, Midway	1980
Portal	Valve Corporation	Valve Corporation, Microsoft Game Studio	2007
Riven	Cyan	Brøderbund, Acclaim Entertainment, Mean Hamster Software	1997
The Secret of Monkey Island	Lucas Film Games	Lucas Arts	1990
SimCity	Maxis, Infogrames, Nintendo EAD, Babaroga	Brøderbund, Maxis, Nintendo, Electronic Arts, Infogrames, Acornsoft	1989
Ultima	Origin Systems, Blue Sky Productions, Looking Glass Studios, Electronic Arts, Bioware Mythic	Origin Systems, Electronic Arts	1981
Warcraft	Blizzard Entertainment	Blizzard Entertainments	1994

APPENDIX 1

Glossary

Activity is a broader term for *task*. Cultural-historical activity theory scholars argue that *activity* is a better description of what the learner actually does, from his or her perspective, in completing a task. In other words, even though there is an instruction-driven objective, the learner might have a different objective in mind for completing the task. (See also *task, instruction-driven, learner-driven.*)

Attendant discourses are sociocultural literacy practices produced and developed by player communities. They exist outside the actual game and may include websites, videos, conferences, or fiction not produced by the original game designers. (See also *interaction.*)

Authenticity refers to the "real" or "natural" quality of a learning resource. Some argue for the superiority of authentic materials, because they were created by and for native or expert speakers, not necessarily for L2TL purposes. Task-based language teaching (TBLT) scholars argue that learning tasks themselves should also be as authentic or as real world as possible. Others note that a learner may have an authentic experience with materials that aren't authentic, and vice versa, and so they argue for the term *genuine* to refer to authentic in the sense of "from the target culture," rather than artificially constructed for L2TL purposes. (See also *task, TBLT.*)

Cognitive interactivity is the interactive quality of a game that immerses players. It is based on visual graphics, sound, and designed narratives. Some game genres, such as interactive fiction, may be more cognitively interactive than other genres, such as action games, because of narrative richness. (See also *context-in-the-game, cultural interactivity, designed narratives, explicit interactivity, flow, functional interactivity, narrative.*)

Comprehensible input refers to input that is delivered to the learner at a level that is understandable and meaningful. According to Krashen's (1984) i + 1 hypothesis, input is most effectively comprehensible when it is delivered at one level above that of the learner. This achieves a balance between challenging learners to understand language above their own level while feeling comfortable with the input they are receiving.

Context is a very broadly defined concept in linguistics. Structural linguists view context as an added layer that is separate from morphosyntax, whereas functionalists view context as inextricable from all instances of language use, and central to its understanding. (See also *functional linguistics, narrative, structural linguistics.*)

Context-in-the-game is our term for the fictional world found in a game, composed of the designed narratives created by the game developers, usually in the form of graphical imagery and language. The context serves to frame the game rules, so that the game can be learned and played. These contexts might be, for example, an alien planet, a haunted mansion, a restaurant, a city, or a farm. (See also *context, context of play, designed narrative.*)

The **context of culture** is a term in functional approaches that refers to the influence of culture on language use on a broader level than context of situation. Situational use is always culturally embedded, and situational features may vary at any level accordingly. (See also *context, context of situation.*)

The **context of play** refers to the world of the player(s), or where, with whom, and for what reasons the game is being played. It is within this context that a gameplay experience becomes meaningful for players, from which their own personal narratives emerge. (See also *context, context-in-the-game, context of situation, personal narrative*.)

The **context of situation** is a term in functional approaches that refers to the potential influence of situation on language use and meaning. Situational features of context may include setting, purpose, speaker intentions, or text type. (See also *context, context of culture, functional linguistics*.)

Cultural interaction refers to the interaction among a game, its players, and broader cultural discourses and communities. It corresponds roughly to interactions *about* a particular game. (See also *attendant discourses, cultural interactivity, textual meaning*.)

Cultural interactivity refers to the quality of a game that gives rise to attendant discourses and interactions about the game, usually outside of the game itself. Game designers have less control over the cultural interactivity of a game than other forms of interactivity, even though the success or popularity of a game may depend on it. (See also *attendant discourses, cognitive interactivity, cultural interaction, explicit interactivity, functional interactivity, interactivity*.)

Cut scenes are narratives that run independently of gameplay, such as small video clips in between, or embedded in, game tasks. Cut scenes serve to ensure that key narratives are presented to all players at particular times, giving the player a sense of temporal progression in the game world. (See also *progression design, quests, spatial and temporal elements*.)

Designed narratives are narrative game elements, including stories, characters, dialogues, and fictional worlds, that a designer creates by means of language, graphics, sounds, and spatial and temporal elements. They comprise the context-in-the-game, contextualize the game rules and structures, and provide players with a sense of cognitive interactivity. They may serve as resources for L2TL. (See also *context-in-the-game, narrative, personal narrative, rules, spatial and temporal elements*.)

A **digital game** is any game that is played through a desktop computer, laptop computer, tablet, game console, handheld game console, or other mobile device. It can be of a variety of genres and types, from action-adventure to simulation-management games, from single to multiplayer, and from mini-games to massively multiplayer online games. (See also *Appendix II*.)

Digital game-mediated second/foreign language teaching and learning (L2TL) refers to the practice of L2TL mediated by activity involving digital games (including video console, web-based, and computer games). The activity does not necessarily have to be with or through the actual game itself but can be around or about the game, too. (See also *attendant discourses, game-based L2TL, game-enhanced L2TL*.)

In digital games, **discernability** refers to a player's ability to determine the outcome of any action. This includes the immediate knowledge of whether or not an action has been successful as well as the relevant feedback necessary to either move forward or complete the failed task. In successful digital games, the majority of outcomes, cues, and resources are salient and immediately recognizable.

Dynamic difficulty assessment (DDA) refers to an emerging type of feedback in digital games specifically suited to single-player experiences. It refers to an automated system of feedback delivery that is adaptive to the skill level of each individual player. In DDA, the game itself adds or eliminates extra cues and resources based on the success or failure of each individual player. (See also *feedback mechanisms, just-in-time*.)

Emergent play happens as a result of the random interactions among player actions and game rules and is not as predictable as linear play. It is more likely to occur in open-ended game design. (See also *linear play, open-ended design*.)

Engagement is the quality of an activity that maintains attention and investment by those participating in it. In games, engagement is what motivates players to interact with digital games in intense ways for long periods of time. Engagement is a complex construct made up of different elements and is representative of the overall gameplay experience many game designers strive for. (See also *flow*.)

Explicit interactivity refers to the designed choices and feedback types provided to players in a game. Some game genres, such as action games, are more explicitly interactive than other genres because of their open-ended designs. (See also *cognitive interactivity, cultural interactivity, discernability, feedback, feedback mechanisms, functional interactivity, interactivity, open-ended design*.)

Extrinsic motivation has its origin outside of the individual. Extrinsic motivation is sometimes equated with reward-driven activity, but it should not be equated with instrumental orientation. (See also *integrative-instrumental orientation*.)

Fail states are a fundamental characteristic of digital games that provide the opportunity for unlimited attempts at success when failure occurs. Combined with complex feedback mechanisms to deliver just-in-time resources, fail states make digital games challenging, repeatable, and motivational. Through fail states, a player is motivated to keep playing and improving to be able to accomplish a task successfully.

Fan art is art created from in-game content. (See also *fan fiction*.)

Fan fiction is created when a player extends the in-game narrative of a digital game. This can include additional storylines, alternate endings, and character additions. (See also *fan art*.)

Feedback refers to the cues and resources a learner is given to aid in language development. Cues and resources can come in a variety of types, including error correction, formative assistance, summative assessment, interactional cues from an interlocutor, metalinguistic discussions, and context. It can occur during activities and interactions as well as after the fact, as is often the case with exams and homework. (See also *feedback as instruction model, feedback mechanisms, just-in-time*.)

The **feedback as instruction model** takes the perspective that feedback is most useful as a developmental tool for ongoing learning, and not primarily as a corrective tool. Feedback as instruction focuses on the delivery of resources and cues when learners need them in order to promote continued L2 development. It is meaningful, relevant, appropriate to the action, and salient to the learner. Digital games are especially effective representations of the feedback as instruction model. (See also *fail states, feedback, just-in-time, zone of proximal development*.)

Feedback mechanisms in this book refer to the techniques used in digital games to provide cues and resources to players. These include leveling, points, asset building, skill building, tips and hints, real-time progress bars, sound effects, and active and in-active game elements. (See also *feedback, negative feedback systems, positive feedback systems*.)

Flow refers to the psychological mindset of a person who is highly involved in an activity (Csikszentmihalyi, 1991). When players achieve a state of flow, they stop being aware of themselves as separate from the action, have complete focus on the task at hand, and often lose track of time. Digital games that encourage flow in players' gameplay experiences have adequate challenges, clear goals, clear feedback, and a sense of control. (See also *engagement.*)

Formal interaction refers to interaction between players and a game. It corresponds roughly to interaction *with* games. (See also *cultural interaction, ideational meaning, social interaction.*)

Functional interactivity refers to the interface of a game, that is, how the player is able to interact with the game by means of the functional interface. A good functionally interactive design will be ergonomic, intuitive, and eventually invisible to the expert player. (See also *cognitive interactivity, cultural interactivity, explicit interactivity, flow, interactivity.*)

Functional linguistics views language meaning as inseparable from language use, and context as central to any understanding of language as a system. Functional approaches are usually able to explain discourse, pragmatics, and social interaction better than formal approaches to linguistics. (See also *context of culture, context of situation, structural linguistics.*)

A **game** is a set of meaningful, sociocultural practices that involve play. It is rule based, has variable outcomes, and differs from other kinds of play in that it is usually goal oriented. (See also *digital game, play.*)

Game-based L2TL refers to the use in L2TL of digital game-based environments designed specifically for the purpose of L2TL. Game-based L2TL offers advantages over game-enhanced L2TL, for example, the capability to target specific learning objectives. (See also *game-based environments, game-enhanced L2TL.*)

Game-based environments for L2TL are educational games designed specifically to teach and promote the learning of second/foreign languages. Although there are still not very many game-based L2TL environments available commercially, the study of digital game-mediated L2TL can inform their future development. (See also *game-based L2TL, vernacular games.*)

Game-enhanced L2TL refers to the use of vernacular digital games for L2TL purposes. Game-enhanced L2TL offers advantages over game-based L2TL, for example, cultural genuineness and the potential for large player communities and attendant discourses. (See also *game-based L2TL, vernacular games.*)

Game literacy is the ability to play, learn through, and understand games. Some researchers suggest that game literacy is a key literacy of the digital age and may enhance a variety of other skills, for example, visualization, abstract thinking, and critical awareness. (See *digital game-mediated L2TL.*)

A **goal** is a purpose or intention for completing a particular activity. In L2TL, goals are usually determined by instructional demands and learner needs, and they inform task objectives. When an activity is directed at a particular goal, it is goal oriented. (See also *activity, goal orienting, instruction-driven, learner-driven, task.*)

Goal orienting is our term for understanding goal orientation as a dynamic and ongoing process, rather than as a static term. Players constantly goal orient while playing, assessing and reassessing their own abilities, risks, challenges, and possible rewards, based on game feedback. (See also *feedback, object-of-the-game.*)

Ideational meaning refers to the explicit semantic meaning of a particular word or utterance. The ideational function of language use is experiential and transactional in nature. (See also *formal interaction, functional linguistics, interpersonal meaning, textual meaning.*)

An **instruction-driven** task is driven by the instructor, learning theory, the curriculum, and assessment demands. The most effective L2TL tasks balance learner-driven with instruction-driven design. (See also *instruction-driven, learner-driven, learning-driven*.)

Integrative-instrumental orientation model refers to Gardner and Lamberts's (1972) model that suggests that learners may have integrative or instrumental reasons for learning an L2. Integrative orientation is a learner's desire to associate with the L2 community on a variety of levels. Instrumental orientation focuses on L2 learning for the attainment of other goals (e.g., getting a better job, making more money, translating research). (See also *L2 motivational self system*.)

Interaction can be defined as reciprocal activity among interlocutors and/or resources in an environment. For example, interaction can occur between a game and a player, among game players, between a learner and a language, or among language users. (See also *feedback, interactivity*.)

Interactivity refers to the qualities of a game that can lead to interaction. Game designers have more control over the interactive aspects of a game than over the interactional aspects, because the latter depend on player agency. (See also *cognitive interactivity, cultural interactivity, explicit interactivity, functional interactivity, interaction*.)

Interpersonal meaning refers to the implicit pragmatic meaning of a particular word or utterance. The interpersonal function of language use is interactional in nature and is dependent on the interlocutors. (See also *functional linguistics, ideational meaning, social interaction, textual meaning*.)

Intrinsic motivation implies doing an activity simply for its own sake. It has its source in the individual completing an activity, rather than from an outside source such as a parent, teacher, grade, or curriculum. (See also *extrinsic motivation*.)

The **just-in-time** concept refers to feedback that is given at just the right moment it is needed, not too soon and not too late. In digital games, the delivery of just-in-time resources is critical to the creation of an enjoyable, balanced gameplay experience, making a game challenging yet playable but not so easy that it is boring. By delivering just-in-time resources, the game itself teaches players to play through their own experiences. (See also *fail states, feedback as instruction model*.)

The **L2 motivational self system model** (Dörnyei, 2005) is a motivational model that entails three components: the ideal L2 self, the ought-to L2 self, and the L2 experience. The ideal L2-self refers to the L2 speaker someone *would like* to become. The ought-to L2 self refers to what someone believes he or she *ought to be* or *ought not to be*. The L2 experience refers to the environments in which the L2 learning is occurring—for example, the classroom, the teacher, peer group, and the curriculum. (See also *integrative-instrumental orientation, process model of learning motivation*.)

Language learning strategies are the conscious thoughts and actions that learners use for L2 learning. These can include learning strategies, performance strategies, and evaluative strategies.

Language play is the ludic, or playful, focus on language form, sometimes separated from its conventional meaning. Language play is found in poetry, rhymes, music, chants, or humor genres. Some researchers speculate that it plays an important role in language learning. (See also *game, play*.)

A **learner-driven** task is directed by the learner, so that he or she is actively aware of his or her role in the activity. Choice and feedback are key elements of a learner-driven task. (See also *goal orienting, instruction driven, learning driven*.)

A **learning-driven** task is designed based on the belief that learning theory can, and should, inform the kinds of learning tasks a learner should perform. Because learning-driven tasks are often driven by assessment demands, they can also lead to learner disengagement. (See also *instruction driven, learner driven.*)

Levels are achievements that signify a player's progression and expertise in a game. They are usually achieved by collecting points, which are won by completing in-game tasks and quests. Tasks are designed for specific levels by being within the capability of players at or around that level. In many games, it becomes increasingly more difficult to achieve a new level as one progresses into higher levels. (See also *feedback as instruction model, scaffolding, zone of proximal development.*)

Linear play is the result of progression-oriented design, in contrast to emergent play. Linear play is predictable, along a path predetermined by the game designers. (See also *emergent play, progression design.*)

Machinima are animated artifacts created by using in-game assets mixed with other media. (See also *fan art, fan fiction.*)

A **narrative** is broadly understood as a way of recounting events in a connected way, such as a story. Narratives are used to relate information and ultimately to teach and transmit culture through processes of contextualization. Narrative is used in game design to contextualize game rules and structures, allowing players to learn and play the game. (See also *context, designed narrative, rules.*)

Negative feedback systems are the feedback systems in digital games that take away certain player advantages in order to re-stabilize the system. Negative feedback systems hold the player back when needed. (See also *positive feedback systems.*)

Negotiation for meaning refers to the activity inherent in communicative interaction that can lead to learning. When an interlocutor does not understand, he or she may ask for clarification or repetition, which leads to negotiation and focus on particular items. (See also *ideational meaning, interaction, interpersonal meaning, textual meaning.*)

The **object of the game** is understood as the means to win or successfully play the game. A player who does not know the object of the game has no rationale for playing it and usually becomes de-motivated. (See also *goal, goal orienting.*)

A game with an **open-ended design** provides players with rules and structures that do not necessarily promote predictable gameplay. There are usually multiple paths to advancement and expertise. Simulation and sandbox games tend to be more open-ended than adventure games, which are more progression oriented in nature. Most games combine open-ended and progression-oriented elements. (See also *emergent play, progression design, rules.*)

Personal narratives are narratives that emerge when a player experiences a game, in a particular context of play, by interacting with the rules and designed narratives of the game, with other players through or around the game, or with attendant discourses about the game. These narratives provide players with a sense of agency and comprise the discourses of player communities. Like designed narratives, they may serve as powerful resources for L2TL. (See also *context of play, designed narratives, narrative.*)

Play is a human activity that may have qualities of mimicry, physical movement, collaboration, competition, and chance. Most importantly, it involves adoption of a particular disposition, on the part of the players, that acknowledges suspension of the conventional rules of time, space, and interaction. (See also *game, language play.*)

Positive feedback systems are the feedback systems in digital games that give additional, advantageous resources to players and, ultimately, interrupt the overall balance of the game system. Positive feedback systems propel the player forward when needed. (See also *negative feedback systems.*)

In Dörnyei's (2001) **process model of learning motivation**, motivation is a dynamic process, involving a particular initial *choice motivation*; investment of time and effort with *executive* motivation; and motivational *retrospection*, which leads to new choices. (See also *integrative-instrumental orientation, L2 motivational self system.*)

In contrast to open-ended design, games with a **progression design**, including most traditional adventure games, tend to be linear, as players progress along a predictable, designed path. Still, players are given relevant choices that have discernable outcomes, even if the eventual outcome is partially predetermined. Game tutorials and lower levels tend toward more progression design, whereas higher levels may be more open-ended. (See also *linear play, open-ended design, rules.*)

A **quest** is a collection of smaller in-game tasks involving a series of challenges, usually with a reward provided for their successful completion. As designed narratives, quests contextualize the game rules. Quests are most often found in action, adventure, and role-play games, especially MMOGs. (See also *context-in-the-game, designed narrative, narrative, task.*)

The **rules** and structures of games are the mechanisms by which a game provides choices, goals, and feedback to players. Rules can combine in open-ended designs to provide emergent play experiences in unpredictable ways, or in progression designs to provide linear play experiences. The rules of a game are contextualized and learned by means of its designed narratives. (See also *designed narrative, emergent play, linear play, narrative, open-ended design, progression design.*)

Scaffolding refers to a pedagogical framework related to the zone of proximal development, which provides learners with feedback at the proper time to achieve optimal development. Scaffolded feedback is individualized, targeted in real time, and delivered as needed based on the interactional situation. Some examples include breaking down complex tasks into simpler tasks, providing organizational tools, offering hints and cues at different levels of detail, and peer group work. (See also *zone of proximal development.*)

Spatial and temporal elements are found in game tasks to provide players with a sense of being part of a fictional world made up of many interrelated narratives. Spatial elements might be buildings, lands, or various places where the game unfolds. Temporal elements put the player in the game space at a particular time, so that the game can unfold in a manner that makes logical sense to the player. (See also *context-in-the-game, designed narrative, personal narrative, quest.*)

Socially informed accounts of L2 learning include sociocultural theory, language socialization, and ecological perspectives. They stress the social aspect of interaction as key to learning and are sometimes contrasted with more psychological-cognitive accounts, which place more emphasis on individual learning. (See also *interaction, functional linguistics, zone of proximal development.*)

Social interaction refers to interaction between or among players during a game. Some multiplayer games are designed to require or encourage social interaction *through* the game itself, whereas with other games, social interaction might happen *around* the game between players in the same physical space or in attendant discourses. (See also *cultural interaction, formal interaction, interpersonal meaning.*)

Structural linguistics views language as the sum of a series of formal yet separate systems, that is, phonology, morphology, syntax, and semantics. Structural linguistics is considered obsolete and has been superseded by cognitive, formal/generative, and functional approaches, although it still influences beliefs and practice in L2TL. (See also *functional linguistics.*)

A **task** is generally understood as a bounded, goal-oriented, learning-focused unit of activity with an outcome that can be measured. Although some researchers disagree on the specific role of tasks in the L2 learning process, most do agree that an L2 learning task should focus primarily on meaning for language use in the real world. (See also *activity, authenticity, goal, task-based language teaching.*)

Task-based language teaching (TBLT) is an approach to L2 pedagogy that uses tasks as an organizational principle. Classroom activity, learning objectives, and assessment measures are structured around tasks. (See also *instruction driven, learner driven, learning driven, task.*)

Textual meaning refers to the discursive meaning of a particular word or utterance, that is, its meaning in relationship to surrounding discourses. Cohesive and discourse markers are key elements of textual meaning. (See also *cultural interaction, functional linguistics, ideational meaning, interpersonal meaning.*)

Vernacular games are digital games not designed for educational purposes. There are thousands of vernacular games, in dozens of languages, in dozens of genres and player configurations. (See also *game-based environments, Appendix II*)

Wraparound activities are learning tasks or pedagogically-mediated activities designed to supplement the tasks and activities built into a game. They are designed by instructors to meet curricular objectives, and may be implemented before, during, and after game-play. (See also *task, activity, quest, game-enhanced L2TL.*).

The **zone of proximal development (ZPD)** is understood as the developmental space between what a learner can do alone and what he or she can do with help. If a learner is able to do an activity with no assistance or unable to do an activity even with help, then that activity is outside his or her ZPD. Ultimately, optimal learning and development occur when instruction targets a learner's ZPD. (See also *feedback as instruction model, scaffolding, socially informed accounts of L2 learning.*)

APPENDIX 2

Guide to Game Types and Genres

Digital games can be categorized according to several typological parameters: **platform** (computer, console, handheld, browser-based, stand-alone, Internet-supported), **cost** (free, purchased, rented, subscription, freemium), **player configuration** (single, multiplayer, massively multiplayer), **type** (traditional, casual, social), and **genre** (action, adventure, role-play, strategy, simulation, other). In this guide, we define and discuss these parameters with regard to their application to game-mediated L2TL. The guide is meant as an introduction to these concepts and does not necessarily indicate the only possible division of game types. It is one organizing principle that will be useful for your understanding of the immense variety of digital game types.

PLATFORM

Digital games are delivered and played through a variety of technology platforms, including personal computers (e.g., desktops, laptops, e-machine), consoles (e.g., Microsoft XBox, Sony Playstation, Nintendo Wii), and mobile devices (e.g., smartphone, Nintendo DS, iPad). Some run on a local hard drive, and others through a browser on the Internet. Games can be either stand-alone, meaning they run locally, or they may have to use the Internet to connect with other players and remote servers hosting game content. For classroom L2TL, some platforms may be precluded because of costs and institutional constraints. Most browser-based games do not need local computer power or separate hardware, only a reliable Internet connection, making them more feasible in some educational contexts. Ideally, an institution would have digital gaming stations with computers and console systems set up in a language learning resource center, with laptops and mobile, handheld technologies available for use by classes.

COMPUTER—Broadly speaking, computer games are digital games that use computer technology. More specifically, however, PC games run off the hard drive of a computer and are usually played via the keyboard and mouse, or sometimes a joystick. Some computer games are very memory and graphics intensive, whereas others are not. These games usually have to be downloaded from the Internet or loaded from a DVD or CD to the computer.

CONSOLE—Console-based games are digital games that run off a dedicated console, such as a *Microsoft XBox*, *Sony PlayStation*, or *Nintendo Wii*. Some games are available in both PC and console versions, and for different console types, but most are specific to one technology or console type. Console games run from purchased or rented discs or they can be downloaded to the console through the user's account. Console games are usually played via various controllers that connect to the console. Some multiplayer console games are Internet-supported and may require subscription fees to the console's online service—Sony does not charge for basic online service to PlayStation users, whereas Microsoft does charge XBox users, although the fees are nominal. Moreover, some console discs will play only in consoles purchased in that country; for example, an XBox console bought in the United States will play only XBox discs bought in the United States, not XBox discs bought in Japan; a PlayStation console bought in the United States will play PlayStation discs bought in either the United States or Japan. Downloaded games can also be restricted by region.

HANDHELD—Handheld games are digital games that run on mobile, handheld devices, some of which, such as a *Nintendo DS*, are like portable mini-consoles, whereas others, such as mobile phones or tablet computers, function as portable, wireless computers. Games on handheld mobiles or tablets are usually downloaded as apps, whereas mini-console games are usually built in or run off game cartridges.

BROWSER-BASED—Many games, especially casual and social games, are browser-based, meaning they are accessed through a browser such as Internet Explorer, Safari, Firefox, or Google Chrome, and they require the use of Flash, Java, or another browser-based technology. Although this means they are online in a technical sense, the term *online* in digital gaming usually means Internet-supported and refers to traditional computer and console games that must be online or have networked connectivity in order to be played.

STAND-ALONE—A stand-alone game is any game designed to be played without an Internet connection. Browser-based, casual games designed for solo players might be miscategorized as stand-alone, but because Internet connectivity is required to run a web browser, they are technically Internet supported.

INTERNET-SUPPORTED—Internet-supported, or online, games require connection to the Internet or a local network to play. All browser-based games are technically Internet-supported. Some multiplayer games can be stand-alone, if the computer or console has multiple controllers, but most are Internet-supported, so that players can play with one another at a distance.

COST

Games can cost anywhere from nothing for basic play on a social network-based casual browser game to upward of $80 for a console disc or download purchased online from another country. It is also important to note that a single copy of a stand-alone game may not allow multiple player accounts; if it does, separate player accounts may not be password protected. Free browser-based games may not require a player login and may not save a player's progress.

Cost should be a consideration in selecting games. For L2TL, games with substantial subscription fees may not be institutionally feasible in some contexts and not an issue in others.

FREE—Many free digital games are available. Many are browser-based and include some social games, casual games, and MMOGs. Some are produced by amateur game designers, but others are relatively high quality and turn profit through advertisements or freemium content. In addition, most games offer a trial version to play for free for a short period of time.

PURCHASED—At the time of publication of this book, the cost to purchase a game costs anywhere from a few U.S. dollars for a casual game, downloaded from the Internet, to US$80 for a traditional console or computer game purchased separately. Most new releases cost about US$40. Older versions of a game will be discounted when a new version is released.

RENTED—Traditional console games can be rented daily, weekly, or monthly, for anywhere from a few U.S. dollars to US$10 or so.

SUBSCRIPTION—Some computer games, such as MMOGs with persistent, changing game worlds, require a monthly subscription fee, upward of US$15 per month for a MMOG such as *World of Warcraft*. Microsoft charges players a subscription fee to play Internet-supported multiplayer console games on its XBox Live online service and to download premium content.

FREEMIUM—The freemium model allows players of free or inexpensive games, usually MMOGs or social games, access to premium content. In a similar setup, Sony allows players to play Internet-supported multiplayer console games on its PlayStation network for free but charges for premium content. In-app purchases are also a common freemium practice. That is, in an app on a mobile device, the player can purchase additional tips or help without interrupting the gameplay experience.

PLAYER CONFIGURATION

Games may allow for solo, multiplayer, or massively multiplayer play in various configurations, sometimes shifting between competition and cooperation among players. In competitive play, players play against one another or against in-game characters or obstacles. In cooperative play, players may play with one another, sometimes together in competition with game characters, obstacles, or other groups of players. As discussed in the chapter on interaction, the predesigned configuration of a game may be adapted with wraparound activities for different classroom and learner configurations.

SINGLE PLAYER—A single-player game is meant to be played by one person interacting with the game content. In multiplayer games, some activities can be done solo, but some may be doable only with one or more other players.

For L2TL, games designed for single players may be adaptable to activities focused on interaction with the game by a single learner or around the game in pairs or groups, but not through the game with other players or learners. Associated communities related to single-player gameplay may also serve as a source of interaction.

MULTIPLAYER—Multiplayer games can be played by two or more players competitively or cooperatively, depending on the game. Players may be at the same console in the same physical space, or they may be at different consoles or computers connected remotely via the Internet, playing in a virtual space. For L2TL, games designed for multiplayer play may be adaptable to activities focused on interaction with the game by a single learner, through the game with other learners or players, or around the game in pairs or groups.

MASSIVELY MULTIPLAYER—In massively multiplayer online games (MMOGs), thousands of players are connected remotely via the Internet, playing in virtual spaces that are persistent, meaning they do not suspend when an individual logs out. Gameplay in MMOGs can be single-player, multiplayer, competitive, or cooperative. In solo or multiplayer games, an L2 teacher could control with whom a student is playing; in most massively multiplayer games, students would be able to play with strangers.

TYPE

Type refers to whether a game is traditional, casual, and/or social. Type is not the same as **genre**, nor is it dependent on **platform**, **player configuration**, or **cost** to play. For L2TL, the potential exists for all types of game, both in game-enhanced contexts using vernacular games and in the design of game-based L2 learning environments.

TRADITIONAL—Traditional digital games run the range of platforms, cost, players, and genres. They are designed to require a time commitment to develop expertise, distinguishing them from casual and most social games, which require less playtime to master the game rules. In this way, they may be called "hardcore," which refers to the dedication required for development of expertise, as opposed to the ease of developing expertise in casual games. Most traditional games allow for dozens of hours of gameplay, and some game worlds are persistent and continually updated, and thus potentially never-ending. Traditional games also offer updated versions or sequels with new content for purchase or, in the case of some Internet-supported games, patches to download, which make smaller and larger changes to gameplay and content.

CASUAL—Casual games are digital games that can be played casually, meaning they do not require as much effort or expertise to play successfully as traditional, hardcore games. The rules of casual games are relatively easy to learn, and they can usually be played intermittently, in small chunks of time, without losing quality of play. Unlike games with large, persistent game worlds, patches, or sequels, they are usually self-contained, meaning they can be finished or "won" in a short period of time, although they are often re-playable—such casual games are sometimes called *mini-games*. Casual games can be of any genre, for example, basic action games such as *Plants vs. Zombies*, dice games such as *Farkle*, management games such as *Diner Dash*, and simulation games such as *Farmville*. They are available for many different platforms and are often browser-based or downloadable and low cost.

SOCIAL—Social games, or more accurately social network games, are usually casual games that integrate social networking technologies into gameplay. They offer in-game resources and play enhancements to players who connect to individuals from their social networks through the game, for example, as "neighbors," "clan members," or "allies," and exchange goods and reciprocate activities with them. Social games often use a freemium model, whereby basic gameplay is free, but access to premium content requires a fee payment. The term *social* can be misleading, because many traditional games (as well as some casual and social games) have large communities of dedicated players who interact socially through the game and around the game with attendant discourses. Additionally, the amount of social interaction required in some social games may be minimal.

GENRE

There are dozens of different game genres, and new ones emerge as existing genres are combined and new technologies are invented. Certain genres may be associated with particular platforms, costs, player configurations, and types, but many genres exist across these parameters. We have identified action, adventure, role-playing, strategy, and simulation/management game genres as being of particular interest to game-mediated L2TL.

Action games

The first videogames were action games, and they are probably what first comes to many minds with the mention of videogames. Action games require the development of physical abilities and eye-hand coordination on a computer keyboard, with a joystick, or with a game console controller. In most action games, players must guide a protagonist or avatar through a fictional world, fighting and outsmarting enemies, to higher levels and greater challenges. There is usually a set progression, and an end state to the game where the player wins. Multiplayer play is sometimes possible, with co-players as teammates or as enemies. Most action games incorporate level and status systems that help players develop expertise.

Many action games incorporate elements from other genres, in particular adventure and role-play games, and there are several different subgenres, elements of which are often combined. These include platform games (e.g., *Super Mario Bros.*), in which players must move and jump among various platforms or levels; maze games (e.g., *PacMan*), in which player must navigate through a maze; and first person shooter games (e.g., *Call of Duty* and *Halo*), in which players use firearms to engage in combat. Sometimes music, dance, and exercise games are also considered action games, although they may incorporate simulation elements as well.

For gaming novices, pure action games may not be as useful for L2TL as other genres, because of time pressures during play and the need to develop physical expertise. However, in sheltered play contexts, and for more expert players, multiplayer team play in action games may give player-learners the opportunity to use an L2 in a meaningful way for genuine social purposes, with real social consequence. Game-enhanced activities around action games might have a pair of player-learners work together, with one playing and the other observing and taking notes on game rules and narratives. The incorporation of action elements into the design of game-based SIEs may make them more exciting and motivating for some players and provide contexts in which time pressures push learners to produce the L2 in meaningful ways.

Adventure games

Adventure games are an established game genre, with roots in interactive storytelling, adventure stories, and mystery novels. In adventure games, a player assumes the role of a protagonist and explores a game world to solve puzzles, collect resources, interact with in-game characters, and complete various intellectual challenges. Gameplay is usually progressive, meaning a player has limited choices and must follow predetermined plotlines, although those are usually branching and often have multiple endings, providing players with a sense of agency and involvement.

Classic adventure games include *Myst* and *Riven*, as well as the *Monkey Island* series. Popular games with adventure elements include *Portal* and *Heavy Rain*. Interactive fiction and visual novels, popular in Asia, are sometimes considered a type of adventure game. Adventure game elements have also informed the concept of quests found in role-playing games (RPGs), but adventure games tend to focus less on action and character development than RPGs. Action-adventure games use adventure elements but involve more physical challenges and may be more quickly paced. The *Legend of Zelda* series is a well-known hybrid action-adventure game.

Adventure games hold much potential for L2TL, for several reasons. First, they are usually rich in narratives and text, often in the form of following directions, learning backstories, and interacting with characters. Most pure adventure games also allow players as much time as they need to make in-game choices. Adventure games tend to be especially focused on problem solving, more so than other genres. Game-enhanced L2TL activities using adventure games would focus on player experiences exploring the game world and solving challenges specifically related to L2 content (e.g., lexicon, skills, cultural knowledge). Designers of game-based L2TL environments might incorporate the rich textual, in-game interactional and narrative elements of adventure games, as well as their branching plot structures, resource collection systems, and problem-solving dynamics.

Role-playing games

Digital role-playing games (RPGs) have their origin in tabletop RPGs such as *Dungeons and Dragons*, in which players developed individualized characters and were led on group quests by game masters. In digital RPGs, a player assumes the role of a character or avatar, but unlike with action and adventure games, the player takes more ownership of the avatar by customizing its characteristics, including its physical and magical abilities and its equipment and gear. Gameplay, which can be solo or with other players, involves exploration of expansive game worlds, completion of quests, and sometimes combat— many RPGs incorporate action and adventure elements. Quests involve mostly intellectual challenges embedded in elaborate game-world narratives, rather than physical challenges, and levels are reached by accumulating experience points, which are awarded for exploring and completing quests. Well-known RPGs include the classics *Ultima*, *Diablo*, and the *Final Fantasy* series.

Massively multiplayer online role-playing games (MMOGs or MMORPGs) are Internet-supported role-playing games that incorporate elements of action and adventure games. MMOGs are highly social, with large communities of players who exchange play strategies and game information outside of the game. Players can join teams and become allies to complete various group and team quests. MMOGs also have their own economies, in which various goods and resources become more or less valuable based on planned scarcity and player trade and production behavior. Well-known MMOGs include *World of Warcraft* and *Everquest*.

For L2TL, RPGs offer the learning potentials of action and adventure games, with the added aspect of character development, which involves meaningful vocabulary use and critical thinking. As with online action games, MMOGs include the potential to interact with expert users of the L2 by teaming up to play the game. In MMORPGs, however, players can be allied with others more permanently. In team gameplay, interaction therefore can have real social consequences, because player reputation in the team may be at stake. For game-enhanced L2TL using MMOGs, players might keep a gaming journal, in which they record their gameplay activity and reflect on it. Designers of game-based L2 learning environments might consider how designs that include character customization, group quests, and resource scarcity can encourage collaboration and competition, thus leading to meaningful interaction.

Strategy games

Strategy games have their origins in traditional games such as chess, in which players spend most of their effort attempting to devise strategies to outwit opponents, whether human or the game itself. The content of digital strategy games is usually history and/or warfare, and they may involve progression-like storylines that unfold as the player discovers, plans, builds, and battles enemies, leading to an end state. They are usually played from a map or top down perspective and have complex interfaces to allow for gameplay management. This perspective allows the player to be omnipresent and make strategy choices based on the overall picture. They are similar to simulation or management games, but unlike games in those genres, strategy games are usually played against other players or the computer itself. Games may be turn-based, first allowing a player to do a series of moves in one turn and then allowing opponents to play their turns, or they may be real-time, meaning players and opponents can make moves any time. Well-known digital strategy games include *Warcraft* and *Civilization*.

Strategy games can be used in L2TL to teach content and vocabulary related to the game topic and may be especially useful for content-based and problem-based language teaching of subjects such as history and geography and skills such as planning and global thinking. In turn-based strategy games, players have plenty of time to plan strategies, consider options, and weigh decisions; for game-enhanced L2TL, these activities can be done as individuals or groups, with supplemental attention to the L2 as needed. For L2TL game design, strategy game principles might be useful for considering how particular designs afford decision making and strategic thinking.

Simulation and management games

Simulation and management (sim/man) games are sometimes not considered games, because they are usually not played with opponents and do not necessarily have end states in which the player wins. The object of a sim/man game is to successfully simulate or manage, for example, a person, group of people, business, farm, city, or planet. In these games, players are gradually given more and more features to manage, sometimes with only a certain amount of resources or within a given time frame. Players develop planning, management, layout, and design skills. Life simulation games allow a player to manage an avatar's life, with detail given to needs such as friendship, employment, health, and nutrition. Sometimes driving, sports, and flight simulation games are also considered within this genre, although there are differences among them. Popular simulation games include the *Sims* series, including *SimCity* and *The Sims*, and the *Tycoon* series. Some social network games such as *Farmville* also fall into the sim/man genre, but they are designed so that players need to exchange resources with other players.

For game-enhanced L2TL, sim/man games might hold potential similar to strategy games, in which game content and vocabulary might be matched with L2TL objectives. Students can also keep gaming journals or write descriptions of their simulated creations. Sim/man games might also be used for critical discussion activities that focus on comparisons between the object of simulation or management and the real-world activity. Sim/man game principles could also be used for simulating interactional dynamics and related pragmatics features.

Other games

Many other game genres may have application to L2TL, for example, digital word games that incorporate crossword, find-a-word, or word scramble elements. These games may have application for learning vocabulary. L2-mediated pair or group activities might also be built around puzzle games that practice logical deduction skills or around chance games involving dice, numbers, and playing cards that practice mathematical and reasoning skills. Such games might also be incorporated as mini-games into the design of game-based L2TL applications.

APPENDIX 3

Digital Game Evaluation Guide for L2 Teaching and Learning

Prior to evaluating any digital game, you should play the game for a minimum of one hour. Two to three hours would be preferable. For game evaluations using this framework, visit http://games2teach.wordpress.com.

1a. Game specifications and parameters

1. Game Title
2. Developer
3. Game Platform
4. Location (e.g., link, purchase site)
5. Cost to Play
6. Player Configuration*
7. Game Type*
8. Game Genre*
9. Summary of Previous Reviews of This Game (e.g., links, key points)
10. Language(s)

*see Appendix 2: Guide to Game Types and Genres for examples.

1b. Game basics

1. In general, what do players do in the game?
2. What is/are the primary object(s) of the game?
3. What is the setting of the game? How does this fit with L2TL objectives?
4. How do players learn to play the game? How difficult is it to play?
5. How does the game teach players how to play? Does this mechanism seem effective? How much language is involved?
6. Approximately how long does it take to reach the end-game point, if there is one?

2. Goals and in-game tasks

1. How is the game divided into in-game tasks and other divisions (e.g., levels, quests, cycles)?
2. How do the separate tasks combine into larger activities?
3. How does the player determine the goals and activities?
4. What does the player have to do to complete the in-game tasks and reach the goals?
5. Are there different ways the player can reach various points in the game and complete different tasks?
6. What language skill areas are used for the in-game tasks? Consider the necessary lexical, grammatical, pragmatic, cultural, and strategic knowledge that is necessary and/or peripheral.
7. How might the above considerations be leveraged for L2 learning activities?

3. Interaction(s)

1. How are interactions with, through, and around the game afforded by the game?
2. Consider the following aspects of cognitive interactivity:
   a. How well does the game environment engage the player?
   b. Describe the graphical and visual feel of the game.
   c. Describe the music and sound of the game.
3. How does the game promote interaction among the players either in or out of the game? If it is a single-player game, how practical would it be to create a pair or group activity around the game?
4. Is there a community of players for this game? If so, what sorts of activities do they engage in? Include relevant links and resources.
5. Does the player feel that his or her choices make a difference in the game?
6. How might the above considerations be leveraged for L2TL?

4. Feedback

1. How does the game provide feedback to players?
2. How many levels of feedback are in the game?
3. Are there other sources of feedback related to the game?
4. How is the feedback individualized for each player?
5. What mediums (i.e., behavioral, image, text based) are used when giving feedback?
6. How might the above considerations be leveraged for L2 learning activities?

5. Game context and narratives

1. What is the context-in-the-game in this game? In other words, what is it about?
2. How does this context fit with L2TL curricular goals (i.e., what type of objectives would best fit with this game)?
3. How are the narratives in the game told or experienced? How do these relate (or not relate) to L2TL?
4. Note some of the specific vocabulary, grammatical, pragmatic, cultural, and strategic knowledge needed to play the game and understand the narratives. Which are most relevant to L2TL?
5. How much knowledge of the in-game narratives is necessary ahead of time to play successfully?
6. Approximately how long does it take to reach the end-game point, if there is one?
7. How appropriate is the language for instructional goals? Where is it most appropriate and inappropriate?

6. Motivation

1. Is this game motivating? In what ways? Do you want to keep playing? Why or why not?
2. Have you/do you experience flow when playing this game? If so, in what way? If not, what could be improved?
3. Is this game engaging? Why or why not?

7a. Summary

1. What are the most relevant aspects of this game as related to L2TL?
2. In what L2TL areas will this game (and its associated attendant discourses) be most relevant?
3. In what L2TL areas will this game (and its associated attendant discourses) be least relevant?
4. Overall, how useful would this game be for the creation and implementation of game-enhanced activities?

7b. Other considerations

1. What are the institutional constraints that might limit (or enhance) the use of this game for L2TL (e.g., lab setting, hardware, software limitations)?
2. What are the contextual/cultural constraints that might limit (or enhance) the use of this game for L2TL (e.g., perceptions, administration, theme of the game)?
3. Is there any other pertinent information related to the use of this game for L2TL?

INDEX

Page numbers followed by f indicate figure.
Page numbers followed by t indicate table.